# THE CONTINENTAL COO BAKING COOKBOOK

The Ultimate Cookie Baking Book with Unique Delightful Flavors, Culture, Traditions, and Stories, from Classic American Chocolate Chip Cookies to the Egyptian Basbousa Cookies

**Milly Cookwell**

# Copyright © 2023 by Milly Cookwell

All rights reserved. No part of this publication may be reproduced, distributed, or transmitted in any form or by any means, including photocopying, recording, or other electronic or mechanical methods, without the prior written permission of the publisher, except in the case of brief quotations embodied in critical reviews and certain other noncommercial uses permitted by copyright law.

## Disclaimer:

The information provided in "The Continental Cookie Baking Cookbook: The Ultimate Cookie Baking Book, with Unique Delightful Flavors, Culture, Traditions, and Stories, from Classic American Chocolate Chip Cookies to the Egyptian Basbousa Cookies" is intended for general informational and educational purposes. While the book aims to provide accurate and reliable information, the author and publisher do not claim or guarantee the suitability, accuracy, or completeness of the content for any specific purpose, and it should not be considered a substitute for professional advice.

The recipes, techniques, and instructions presented in this cookbook are based on the author's experience and research. However, individual results may vary, and the author and publisher are not responsible for any adverse outcomes or accidents that may occur during the preparation and consumption of the recipes.

Readers are encouraged to use their discretion and judgment when following the recipes, especially if they have allergies, dietary restrictions, or health concerns. It is advisable to consult with a qualified professional for personalized advice regarding dietary, nutritional, or health-related matters.

The author and publisher of "The Continental Cookie Baking Cookbook" disclaim any liability for damages or losses, including but not limited to any direct, indirect, consequential, or incidental damages, that may result from the use of the information provided in this book. The author and publisher shall not be held responsible for any health issues or adverse effects that may arise from the consumption of the cookies or ingredients presented in the book.

Incorporating external ingredients, tools, and equipment, or any modifications to the recipes are at the reader's discretion and risk. The author and publisher are not responsible for any consequences that may arise from such modifications.

While the book may suggest ingredient substitutions and variations, it is the reader's responsibility to ensure that these modifications are suitable for their specific dietary needs and preferences. Always read ingredient labels and follow recommended safety precautions.

By using this cookbook, readers acknowledge and agree to assume all responsibility and risks associated with their use of the information presented within. The author and publisher do not endorse any specific products, brands, or manufacturers mentioned in the book and are not responsible for any changes or discontinuations of such products.

The content in this book is protected by copyright law. Reproduction, distribution, or use of any part of this book for commercial purposes or without proper attribution is strictly prohibited.

By purchasing and using "The Continental Cookie Baking Cookbook," readers are accepting the terms and conditions outlined in this disclaimer. Readers are encouraged to reach out to the author or publisher with any questions or concerns related to the book.

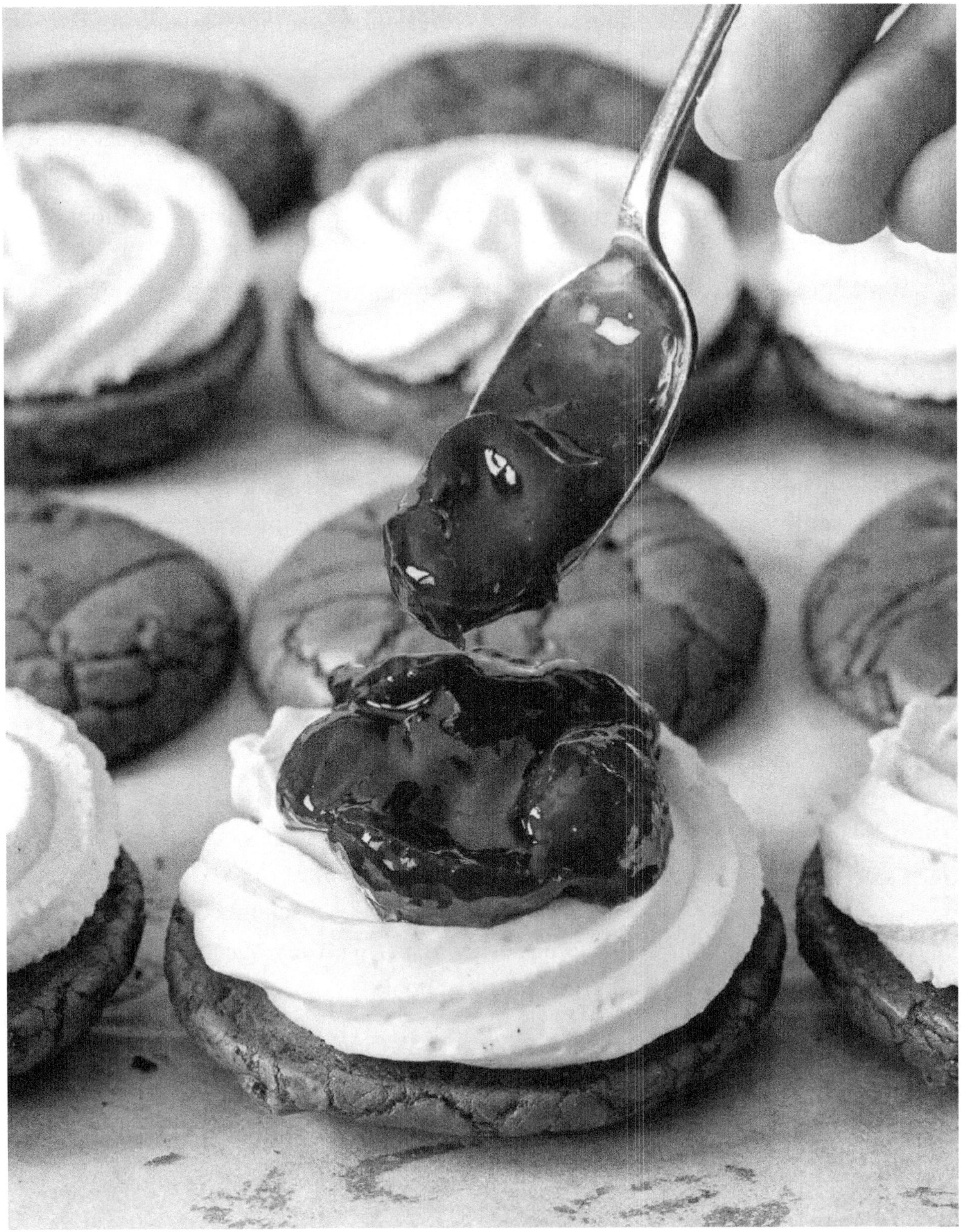

# TABLE OF CONTENT

## HOW TO USE THIS BOOK..............................9
## INTRODUCTION........................................10
## GENERAL BAKING TIPS..............................11
## CHAPTER 1: NORTH AMERICAN COOKIE DELIGHTS....................................................13
Classic American Chocolate Chip Cookies......... 13
Maple Pecan Cookies from Canada................... 14
Mexican Wedding Cookies............................... 15
Cranberry White Chocolate Cookies from New England................................................... 16
Oatmeal Raisin Cookies................................... 17
Peanut Butter Cookies..................................... 18
Snickerdoodles............................................... 19
White Chocolate Macadamia Nut Cookies.......... 20
Molasses Cookies........................................... 21
Ranger Cookies.............................................. 22

## CHAPTER 2: SOUTH AMERICAN COOKIE SENSATIONS..............................................23
Alfajores from Argentina................................. 23
Cocadas Cookies............................................ 24
South American Rosquillas.............................. 25
Tortas Negras................................................ 26

Bolachas de Maizena............................................27
Canestrelli........................................................28
Brazilian Empanadas.........................................29
Hojarascas.......................................................30
Sequilhos Cookies.............................................31
Brazilian Brigadeiros Cookies............................32
Peruvian Polvorones Cookies...........................33
Colombian Arequipe Thumbprint Cookies..........34

## CHAPTER 3: EUROPEAN COOKIE ELEGANCE.35
French Macarons with Various Fillings...............35
Italian Amaretti Cookies....................................36
German Lebkuchen Cookies.............................37
Spanish Almond Tuiles......................................38
Russian Tea Cakes...........................................39
Italian Biscotti:..................................................40
Linzer Cookies:.................................................42
Speculoos (Belgium/Netherlands).....................43
Italian Pizzelle..................................................44
French Palmiers...............................................45
Norwegian Krumkake Cookie............................46

## CHAPTER 4: ASIAN COOKIE EXTRAVAGANZA 47
Chinese Almond Cookies..................................47
Japanese Matcha Shortbread...........................48
Indian Nan Khatai.............................................49

Thai Mango Sticky Rice Cookies......................50
Filipino Polvorón...........................................51
Korean Yakgwa............................................ 52
Indonesian Kue Lidah Kucing........................53
Taiwanese Pineaple Cakes........................... 54
Vietnamese Sesame Peanut Candy (Keo Me Phung)..........................................................55
Malaysian Kuih Bangkit.................................56
Japanese Dorayaki.......................................57
Chinese Mooncakes.....................................58

## CHAPTER 5: AFRICAN COOKIE ADVENTURES 60
Moroccan Almond Crescents........................ 60
South African Hertzog Cookies...................... 61
Egyptian Basbousa Cookies......................... 62
Nigerian Chin-Chin....................................... 63
Ma'amoul (North Africa)................................64
Kahk (Egyptian Eid Cookie):......................... 65
Biskut Kenyah (Kenya):................................ 66
Koeksisters (South Africa)............................ 67
Namibian Ginger Biscuits............................. 69
Mandazi (East Africa)................................... 70
Kulikuli (West Africa).................................... 71
Baklava (North Africa).................................. 72
Kletskoppen (South Africa)...........................73

## CHAPTER 6: OCEANIC COOKIE BLISS............74

Australian Anzac Biscuits..................................74
New Zealand Kiwi Shortbread...........................75
Hawaiian Coconut Macadamia Cookies.............76
Fijian Taro Root Cookies................................... 78

## CHAPTER 7: ANTARCTICA-INSPIRED ICEBOX COOKIES..................................................... 79
Iced Blueberry Glacier Cookies..........................79
Polar Bear Pawprint Cookies............................. 80
Snowflake Cookies............................................ 81

## CONVERSION CHART......................................82
Volume Measurements:......................................82
Weight Measurements:.......................................82
Temperature Conversions:................................. 82
Common Ingredient Conversions:......................82
Baking Substitutions...........................................82

## LIST OF INGREDIENTS.................................... 83
## TOOLS, EQUIPMENTS AND MATERIALS...........85
## 30 COOKIE BAKING "MASTER" TIPS................87
## CONCLUSION....................................................89
## BONUS: BEGINNER'S GUIDE TO COOKIE DECORATING TECHNIQUES............................ 91

8

# HOW TO USE THIS BOOK

This section will help you make the most of this cookbook and explore the diverse range of cookies it offers.

***Getting Started:*** Begin by reading the introduction to familiarise yourself with the concept and purpose of the book.
Take note of the prep time, cooking time, and yields mentioned at the beginning of each recipe to plan your baking session accordingly.

***Ingredient Preparation:*** Before starting any recipe, gather all the ingredients listed in the specific recipe you wish to bake. Refer to the comprehensive list of ingredients in the book's appendix if you need to check for any substitutes or alternatives.

***Recipe Selection:*** Flip through the chapters to explore the cookies from different continents. You can choose to follow the recipes chronologically or jump to any continent that piques your interest. Each chapter is dedicated to one continent, making it easy to navigate and find recipes that suit your preferences.

***Recipe Details:*** Once you've selected a recipe, read through it carefully to understand the steps, measurements, and any optional ingredients. Note any special techniques or tips provided in the recipe introduction or along the way. These insights can be valuable for achieving the best results.

***Baking Process:*** Follow the step-by-step directions in each recipe, paying attention to details such as mixing, baking times, and temperatures.
Feel free to adapt the recipes to your taste preferences, such as adjusting sweetness levels, adding extra spices, or incorporating unique ingredients.

***Creativity and Presentation:*** "The Continental Cookie Baking" encourages creativity in your cookie presentation and decoration. Experiment with different shapes, colours, and toppings to make your cookies unique.

***Dietary Considerations:*** Keep in mind that some recipes may require substitutions or modifications to accommodate dietary restrictions. The baking substitutions chart in the book's appendix can be a helpful reference.

***Explore and Share:*** As you bake your way through the book, take the opportunity to learn about the cultural and culinary aspects of each continent. Let the stories and flavours transport you.
Share your cookies with friends and family, and share the joy of this global culinary adventure.

***Revisit and Experiment:*** Don't hesitate to revisit your favourite recipes or experiment with variations to create your signature cookies inspired by different continents.
Keep the book handy as a reference for future baking endeavours and continue to explore the world of cookies.

# INTRODUCTION

I introduce you to the enchanting world of cookies, a realm where sugar, flour, and a pinch of love come together to create tiny bites of happiness that transcend borders and cultures. In this book, "The Continental Cookie Baking," I invite you on a delightful journey through the seven continents, where we'll explore a vast array of cookie recipes that reflect the unique flavours, traditions, and stories of each region.

For me, cookies have always been more than just a baked treat. They are vessels of nostalgia, comfort, and creativity. As a professional chef and avid traveller, I've had the privilege of experiencing the world's diverse culinary traditions. From the bustling markets of Marrakech, where the scent of Moroccan almond crescents fills the air, to the serene tea houses of Kyoto, where matcha shortbread melts in your mouth, I've witnessed how cookies can tell stories of people, places, and history.

The idea for this book came to me during a chilly winter evening in my kitchen. As I baked a batch of classic American chocolate chip cookies, I couldn't help but wonder about the stories these cookies held. The warm, buttery aroma wafting through my home reminded me of my grandmother, who used to bake these cookies for me as a child. I realised that cookies have the power to connect us to our past, transport us to distant lands, and ignite our imaginations.

Our journey begins with North America, where iconic cookies like chocolate chip cookies have become a symbol of home and comfort. These cookies have been shared by generations around the world, and there's something incredibly heartwarming about their simplicity and universality. As you bake them, you'll feel the warmth of a cosy American kitchen, even if you're halfway across the globe.

South America introduces us to a kaleidoscope of flavours, from the sweet dulce de leche-filled alfajores of Argentina to the fudgy Brazilian brigadeiros. These cookies are a testament to the continent's vibrant culture and love for celebration. Imagine yourself dancing at a lively Brazilian carnival while savouring the sweet indulgence of brigadeiros.

In Europe, we delve into a world of sophistication and elegance with cookies like French macarons and Italian amaretti. These delicate treats have graced the tables of royalty and continue to enchant us with their artful craftsmanship. Baking European cookies is like taking a journey through centuries of culinary refinement.

The Asian continent offers a fascinating blend of flavours, from the nutty Chinese almond cookies to the earthy matcha shortbread of Japan. These cookies reflect the deep-rooted traditions and modern innovations of Asian cuisine. With each bite, you'll embark on a sensory voyage to bustling markets and serene tea gardens.

Africa introduces us to the rich and diverse flavours of the continent, from the aromatic Moroccan almond crescents to the sweet nostalgia of South African Hertzog cookies. These cookies tell stories of resilience, resourcefulness, and the vibrant tapestry of African cultures. They are a reminder of the power of community and connection.

Our journey takes an unexpected twist as we explore the icy terrain of Antarctica. Here, we'll discover the world of icebox cookies, perfect for chilling and sharing on a hot summer's day or any day when you need a cool treat. These cookies offer a unique blend of flavours inspired by the frozen continent.

Finally, in Oceanic Cookie Bliss, we'll traverse the stunning landscapes of Australia, New Zealand, Hawaii, and Fiji through cookies that capture the essence of the islands. From Anzac biscuits to Kiwi shortbread, these cookies evoke images of pristine beaches, lush rainforests, and warm island hospitality.

As we embark on this sweet adventure through the seven continents, I encourage you to not only follow the recipes but also infuse your own creativity and love into each batch. Experiment with flavours, shapes, and decorations, and share your creations with family and friends. Let cookies be the bridge that connects you to the world, one delectable bite at a time.

So, tie on your apron, preheat your oven, and get ready to explore the rich tapestry of flavours that our world has to offer through "The Continental Cookie Baking." Together, we'll discover the joy of baking and the sweet stories that unite us all.

## GENERAL BAKING TIPS

*Measure Accurately:*
Baking is a precise science, so it's crucial to measure your ingredients accurately. Use dry measuring cups for dry ingredients like flour and sugar and liquid measuring cups for wet ingredients like milk or oil.

*Room Temperature Ingredients:*
Many recipes call for ingredients like butter, eggs, and milk to be at room temperature. This ensures even mixing and better results. Plan ahead and let them sit out for about 30 minutes before baking.

*Preheat the Oven:*
Always preheat your oven to the specified temperature in the recipe before placing your cookies inside. This helps ensure even baking.

*Use Quality Ingredients:*
High-quality ingredients can make a significant difference in the taste and texture of your cookies. Invest in good butter, fresh eggs, and pure extracts for the best results.

*Sift Dry Ingredients:*
Sifting dry ingredients like flour, baking powder, and cocoa powder helps break up lumps and ensures even distribution in your dough.

*Don't Overmix:*
Overmixing can lead to tough cookies. To prevent overworking the dough, only mix

the ingredients until they are barely incorporated.

***Chill the Dough:*** When the recipe calls for it, chill the dough before baking. This helps cookies maintain their shape and prevents excessive spreading in the oven.

***Properly Space Cookies:*** Leave enough space between cookies on the baking sheet to allow for spreading. Follow the recipe's instructions regarding spacing.

***Rotate Baking Sheets:*** If you're baking multiple sheets of cookies at once, rotate the sheets halfway through the baking time to ensure even browning.

***Check for Doneness:*** Cookies continue to bake slightly after you remove them from the oven due to residual heat. Be mindful not to overbake; cookies should be slightly golden at the edges and still soft in the centre.

***Cool Properly:*** Allow cookies to cool on the baking sheet for a few minutes before transferring them to a wire rack to cool completely. They won't disintegrate while they're still heated because of this.

***Experiment and Have Fun:*** Baking is an art as well as a science. Don't be afraid to experiment with flavours, shapes, and decorations to make the recipes your own.

***Learn from Mistakes:*** Baking is a learning process. If a batch doesn't turn out as expected, don't be discouraged. Analyse what went wrong and use that knowledge to improve in your next attempt.

***Keep Records:*** Consider keeping a baking journal to note any modifications, substitutions, or personal tips for each recipe. This can be invaluable for future baking endeavours.

***Enjoy the Process:*** Baking is a joyous and creative activity. Savour the experience, and don't forget to enjoy the delicious results of your hard work.

# CHAPTER 1: NORTH AMERICAN COOKIE DELIGHTS

## Classic American Chocolate Chip Cookies

These cookies have been a staple in American households for generations, and I have fond memories of my grandmother baking them for me. The perfect blend of buttery richness and sweet chocolate chips makes them a beloved treat for all ages.

**Prep Time: 15 mins**
**Cooking Time: 10-12 mins**
**Yields: 24 cookies**

*Ingredients:*
1 cup (2 sticks) unsalted butter, softened
3/4 cup granulated sugar
3/4 cup brown sugar, packed
2 large eggs
1 teaspoon pure vanilla extract
2 1/4 cups all-purpose flour
1 teaspoon baking soda
1/2 teaspoon salt
2 cups semisweet chocolate chips

*Directions:*
- Preheat your oven to 350°F (180°C). Line two baking sheets with parchment paper or silicone baking mats. This ensures that your cookies won't stick to the pan and facilitates even baking.

- In a large mixing bowl, cream together the softened butter, granulated sugar, and brown sugar until the mixture is light and fluffy. This usually takes about 2-3 minutes using an electric mixer or a wooden spoon.

- Add the eggs one at a time, mixing well after each addition. Then, stir in the vanilla extract until it's well incorporated into the mixture.

- In a separate bowl, whisk together the all-purpose flour, baking soda, and salt. Gradually add this dry mixture to the wet ingredients, mixing until just combined. Be careful not to overmix, as this can lead to tougher cookies.

- Gently fold in the semisweet chocolate chips until they are evenly distributed throughout the cookie dough. You can use as many or as few chocolate chips as you like, depending on your preference for chocolate intensity.

- Using a spoon or cookie scoop, drop rounded tablespoons of cookie dough onto the prepared baking sheets, spacing them about 2 inches apart. This allows room for the cookies to spread as they bake.

- Place the baking sheets in the preheated oven and bake for 10-12 minutes or until the edges of the cookies are lightly golden brown, but the centres are still soft. Remember that cookies continue to cook a bit after you take them out of the oven due to residual heat, so it's okay if they appear slightly undercooked.

- Remove the cookies from the oven and let them cool on the baking sheets for a few minutes before transferring them to wire racks to cool completely. This helps them set up without becoming too crispy. Once cooled, savour the simple joy of a Classic American Chocolate Chip Cookie, whether it's with a glass of cold milk or as a delightful snack.

## Maple Pecan Cookies from Canada

The delightful Maple Pecan Cookies from Canada – a true testament to the country's love affair with maple syrup and its lush forests. The combination of buttery pecans and the rich, earthy sweetness of pure maple syrup.

**Prep Time: 15 minutes**
**Cooking Time: 12-15 minutes**
**Yield: 24 cookies**

*Ingredients:*
1 cup (2 sticks) unsalted butter, softened
1/2 cup pure maple syrup (make sure it's the real deal!)
1/2 cup granulated sugar
1/2 cup brown sugar, packed
2 large eggs
1 teaspoon pure vanilla extract
2 1/2 cups all-purpose flour
1 teaspoon baking soda
1/2 teaspoon salt
1 cup chopped pecans
Optional: Maple sugar for dusting (for that extra maple kick!)

*Directions:*
- Set the oven's temperature to 350°F (175°C). Use parchment paper to line a baking sheet or gently oil it.
- Softened butter, granulated sugar, and brown sugar are combined in a large mixing basin and creamed until frothy and light. It ought should take two to three minutes.
- One at a time, add the eggs, making sure to completely integrate each before continuing. Add the vanilla essence and stir.
- The all-purpose flour, baking soda, and salt should be combined in a separate basin. Mix until just mixed after gradually adding the dry mixture to the butter and sugar mixture. If you want delicate cookies, don't overmix.
- Gently fold in the chopped pecans, distributing them evenly throughout the dough.
- Scoop out tablespoon-sized portions of dough and roll them into balls. Place the

dough balls on the prepared baking sheet, leaving some space between each for spreading.
- For an extra maple flavour and a touch of sweetness, you can lightly sprinkle each cookie with maple sugar before baking.
- Bake the cookies in the preheated oven for 12-15 minutes, or until they are golden brown around the edges but still slightly soft in the centre.
- After the cookies have finished cooling on the baking sheet for a few minutes, move them to a wire rack to finish cooling. This will help them firm up while maintaining a chewy centre.
- Once cooled, these Maple Pecan Cookies are ready to enjoy. Pair them with a hot cup of Canadian maple-flavoured coffee or a glass of cold milk for the ultimate Canadian cookie experience.

## Mexican Wedding Cookies

Blend of toasted nuts, buttery goodness, and a dusting of powdered sugar left a lasting impression.

**Prep Time: 20 minutes**
**Cooking Time: 12-15 mins**
**Cooling Time: 30 mins**

*Ingredients:*
Unsalted butter, 1 cup (2 sticks), at room temperature
Extra sugar can be used for dusting.
1 teaspoon pure vanilla extract
2 cups all-purpose flour
1/2 cup finely chopped toasted pecans or almonds
1/4 teaspoon salt

*Directions:*
- Preheat your oven to 325°F (160°C).
Use silicone baking mats or parchment paper to line a baking pan.
- In a mixing bowl, beat the softened butter and 1/2 cup of powdered sugar together until creamy and smooth. This may take about 2-3 minutes of mixing.
- Mix in the vanilla extract and salt until well combined.
- Slowly add the flour to the mixture, one cup at a time, mixing until the dough comes together. Be careful not to overmix; stop as soon as the dough is formed.
- Gently fold in the finely chopped toasted pecans or almonds into the dough. This will add a delightful nutty crunch to your cookies.
- Scoop out small portions of dough and roll them into 1-inch (2.5 cm) balls. They should be separated from one another as you arrange them on the prepared baking sheet.
- Bake in the preheated oven for 12-15 minutes, or until the cookies are just set and the bottoms are lightly golden. The cookies may still be pale on top.
- After the cookies have cooled slightly on the baking sheet, move them to a wire rack to finish cooling. Once the cookies are completely cool, generously dust them with

powdered sugar. This step adds a sweet, snowy finish to your Mexican Wedding Cookies.
- Your Mexican Wedding Cookies are now ready to enjoy. Serve them with a cup of tea or coffee, and savour the nutty, buttery bliss of this beloved Mexican treat.

## Cranberry White Chocolate Cookies from New England

These cookies encapsulate the essence of the region with every sweet, tangy, and creamy bite.

**Prep: 15 mins**
**Chill: 30 mins**
**Bake: 12-15 mins**

*Ingredients:*
1 cup (2 sticks) unsalted butter, softened
1 cup granulated sugar
2 large eggs
2 teaspoons pure vanilla extract
2 ½ cups all-purpose flour
1 teaspoon baking powder
½ teaspoon baking soda
½ teaspoon salt
1 cup dried cranberries
1 ½ cups white chocolate chips

*Directions:*
- In a large mixing bowl, cream together the softened butter and granulated sugar until light and fluffy, about 2 minutes.
- Add the eggs one at a time, thoroughly blending between additions. Add the vanilla essence and stir.
- Mix the flour, baking soda, baking powder, and salt in a another basin. Mixing until just incorporated, gradually add this dry mixture to the wet components.
- Spread the white chocolate chips and dried cranberries equally throughout the dough by gently folding them in.
- Refrigerate the cookie dough for at least 30 minutes after covering it with plastic wrap. The cookies won't stretch out too much when baked with the dough chilled.
- Set a baking sheet on your oven's 350°F (175°C) rack and preheat the oven.
- Scoop rounded tablespoons of chilled cookie dough onto the prepared baking sheet, leaving enough space between each cookie to allow for spreading.
- Bake in the preheated oven for 12-15 minutes, or until the edges turn golden brown and the centres are slightly soft but set.
- Take the cookies out of the oven and allow them to cool for a few minutes on the baking sheet before transferring them to a wire rack to finish cooling.
- Once cooled, savour the delightful combination of tart cranberries and creamy white chocolate that captures the essence of New England's autumn charm. Serve with a glass of cold milk or a warm cup of tea.

# Oatmeal Raisin Cookies

The North American Oatmeal Raisin Cookie – a timeless classic. These chewy, hearty cookies are the epitome of homey comfort, conjuring memories of childhood and cosy afternoons with a glass of milk. Simplicity can create the most extraordinary flavours, and these cookies are a testament to that belief.

**Prep Time: 15 mins**
**Cooking Time: 15 mins**

### *Ingredients*
1 cup (2 sticks) unsalted butter, softened
1 cup granulated sugar
1 cup packed light brown sugar
2 large eggs
1 teaspoon pure vanilla extract
1 1/2 cups all-purpose flour
1 teaspoon baking soda
1 teaspoon ground cinnamon
1/2 teaspoon salt
3 cups old-fashioned rolled oats
1 1/2 cups raisins

### *Directions:*
- Set the oven's temperature to 350°F (175°C). Two baking pans should be lightly greased or lined with parchment paper.
- The softened butter, granulated sugar, and light brown sugar should be thoroughly mixed and smooth in a large mixing basin. It should just take a few minutes to do this.
- One at a time, add the eggs, making sure to completely integrate each before continuing. Pure vanilla essence should be added until the batter is flavorful.
- The all-purpose flour, baking soda, ground cinnamon, and salt should be combined in a separate basin.
- Gradually add the dry ingredients into the wet mixture, stirring until everything is just combined. Be careful not to overmix; you want a cookie dough that's uniform but not tough.
- Gently fold in the old-fashioned rolled oats and raisins until they are evenly distributed throughout the dough. The oats give the cookies their delightful chewiness, and the raisins add bursts of sweet flavour.
- Using a spoon or cookie scoop, drop rounded tablespoons of cookie dough onto your prepared baking sheets, spacing them about 2 inches apart to allow room for spreading during baking.
- Slide the baking sheets into the preheated oven and bake for 12-15 minutes or until the edges are golden brown and the centres are still slightly soft. Always keep in mind that the cookies will continue to set up as they cool.
- Remove the cookies from the oven and let them cool on the baking sheets for a few minutes before transferring them to a wire rack to cool completely. As they cool, the flavours will meld, creating that perfect blend of chewiness and sweetness.

# Peanut Butter Cookies

Their nutty flavour and crumbly texture have made them a timeless classic that's beloved by people of all ages.

**Prep Time: 15 mins**
**Cooking Time: 12 mins**
**Yields: 24 cookies**

*Ingredients:*
1 cup (2 sticks) unsalted butter, softened
1 cup creamy peanut butter
1 cup granulated sugar
1 cup packed light brown sugar
2 large eggs
1 teaspoon pure vanilla extract
2 1/2 cups all-purpose flour
1 1/2 teaspoons baking soda
1 teaspoon baking powder
1/2 teaspoon salt

*Directions:*
- Preheat your oven to 350°F (175°C). Line baking sheets with parchment paper or lightly grease them.
- In a large mixing basin, combine the softened butter, light brown sugar, and granulated sugar and beat until fluffy. When using an electric mixer, this should take two to three minutes.
- To the butter and sugar mixture, add the creamy peanut butter. Combine well after mixing.
- One at a time, beat in the eggs, making sure each is well mixed before adding the next. Add the pure vanilla extract after that.
- The all-purpose flour, baking soda, baking powder, and salt should be combined in a separate basin.
- In the big mixing bowl, gradually add the dry ingredient combination to the wet components. Mix until just combined. Be careful not to overmix; the dough should be cohesive but not overly stiff.
- Using a spoon or your hands, scoop out portions of dough and roll them into 1.5-inch (4 cm) balls. Place them on the prepared baking sheets, leaving enough space between each for the cookies to spread while baking.
- Using a fork, gently press down on each cookie, creating a crosshatch pattern on the surface. You can dip the fork in a little sugar before each press to prevent sticking.
- Bake the cookies in the preheated oven for 10-12 minutes or until they are lightly golden around the edges. The cookies will continue to firm up as they cool, so don't over bake if you prefer a soft and chewy texture.
- Allow the peanut butter cookies to cool on the baking sheets for a few minutes before transferring them to wire racks to cool completely. Once cooled, savour the delicious nostalgia of homemade peanut butter cookies with a glass of milk or your favourite beverage.

# Snickerdoodles

**Prep Time: 15 mins**
**Cooking Time: 12 mins**
**Yields: 24 cookies**

*Ingredients:*
**For the Cookie Dough:**
1 cup (2 sticks) unsalted butter, softened
1 1/2 cups granulated sugar
2 large eggs
2 3/4 cups all-purpose flour
2 teaspoons cream of tartar
1 teaspoon baking soda
1/4 teaspoon salt

**For the Cinnamon-Sugar Coating:**
1/4 cup granulated sugar
1 1/2 tablespoons ground cinnamon

*Directions:*
- Start by preheating your oven to 375°F (190°C) and lining a baking sheet with parchment paper. This will ensure that your Snickerdoodles bake evenly and don't stick to the pan.
- In a large mixing basin, combine 1 1/2 cups of granulated sugar with the softened butter and beat until frothy. This step is necessary to get that delicious Snickerdoodle texture.
- One at a time, beat in the eggs, making sure each is well mixed before adding the next. Your cookies will have a delicate crumb and a lovely, golden color as a result.
- In a separate bowl, sift together the all-purpose flour, cream of tartar, baking soda, and salt. Sifting helps prevent lumps and ensures even distribution of the leavening agents.
- Mix the wet components first, then gradually add the dry ingredients, blending until just incorporated. Be careful not to overmix, as this can lead to tough cookies. The dough should be soft and slightly sticky.
- In a small bowl, combine the remaining 1/4 cup of granulated sugar and the ground cinnamon for the coating. Shape the dough into 1-inch balls and roll each ball in the cinnamon-sugar mixture until evenly coated.
- Arrange the coated dough balls on the prepared baking sheet, spacing them about 2 inches apart to allow room for spreading during baking.
- Bake the Snickerdoodles in the preheated oven for 10 to 12 minutes or until they are golden around the edges but still slightly soft in the centre. Remember that cookies continue to cook a bit after they're taken out of the oven, so don't over bake if you want that chewy texture.
- Once baked, let the Snickerdoodles cool on the baking sheet for a few minutes before transferring them to a wire rack to cool completely. This will allow them to set and develop that perfect texture. Then, savour each bite of these delightful cinnamon-sugar-coated cookies.

# White Chocolate Macadamia Nut Cookies

White Chocolate Macadamia Nut Cookies are a perfect marriage of creamy white chocolate and crunchy macadamia nuts, resulting in a sublime combination of flavours and textures.

**Prep Time: 15 mins**
**Cooking Time: 14 mins**
**Yields: 24 cookies**

## *Ingredients:*
1 cup (2 sticks) unsalted butter, softened
1 cup granulated sugar
2 large eggs
1 teaspoon pure vanilla extract
2 1/4 cups all-purpose flour
1/2 teaspoon baking soda
1/2 teaspoon salt
White chocolate chunks or chips, 1 1/2 cups
Macadamia nuts, one cup, coarsely chopped

## *Directions:*
- Pre-heat your oven to 350 degrees Fahrenheit (175 degrees Celsius), and line baking pans with parchment paper.
- Cream the softened butter and granulated sugar in a large mixing basin until the mixture is frothy and light. It ought should take two to three minutes.
- Before adding the next egg, make sure the previous one is well absorbed. Beat in the eggs one at a time. Add the vanilla extract next, and blend thoroughly.
- The all-purpose flour, baking soda, and salt should be combined in a separate basin.
- The dry ingredients should be added gradually to the butter and sugar combination. Mix until just combined. Be careful not to overmix; you want the dough to come together without being overworked.
- Gently fold in the white chocolate chips or chunks and the chopped macadamia nuts. Make sure they are dispersed equally throughout the dough.
- Place the cookie dough portions, which should be about 1.5 inches in diameter, on the preheated baking sheets using a cookie scoop or a spoon. Each cookie needs ample room between them since they expand out while baking.
- Bake in the preheated oven for 12-14 minutes, or until the edges of the cookies turn a light golden brown. The centres should still be slightly soft, as they will continue to set as they cool.
- Allow the cookies to cool on the baking sheets for a few minutes before transferring them to a wire rack to cool completely. Once cooled, indulge in the irresistible combination of white chocolate and macadamia nut goodness.

## Molasses Cookies

**Prep Time: 15 mins**
**Cooking Time: 12 mins per batch**
**Yields: 36 cookies**

*Ingredients:*
2 1/4 cups all-purpose flour
2 teaspoons baking soda
1/2 teaspoon salt
1 1/2 teaspoons ground ginger
1 teaspoon ground cinnamon
1/2 teaspoon ground cloves
1/2 cup unsalted butter, softened
1/4 cup vegetable shortening
1 cup granulated sugar
1/4 cup dark molasses
1 large egg
1 teaspoon pure vanilla extract
Granulated sugar for rolling

*Directions:*
- Set your oven at 350 degrees Fahrenheit (175 degrees Celsius) and line two baking sheets with parchment paper.
- Mix the flour, baking soda, salt, ginger, cinnamon, and cloves in a medium bowl. Set this dry mixture aside.
- In a separate large mixing bowl, beat together the softened butter, vegetable shortening, and 1 cup of granulated sugar until the mixture is creamy and smooth. This should take about 2-3 minutes.
- Add the dark molasses, egg, and pure vanilla extract to the sugar-butter mixture. Beat until well combined.
- Gradually add the dry mixture to the wet mixture, mixing until the dough comes together. Be careful not to overmix; you want a uniform dough, not an overworked one.
- Scoop out portions of dough and roll them into 1-inch balls. Each ball is equally coated after being rolled in granulated sugar.
- On the prepared baking sheets, arrange the sugared dough balls, leaving space between them to allow for spreading while baking.
- When the edges of the cookies are firm but the centres are still somewhat soft, bake them in the preheated oven for 10 to 12 minutes. As they cool, the cookies will continue to solidify.
- After baking, let the cookies cool for a few minutes on the baking sheets before moving them to wire racks to finish cooling.
- Store your molasses cookies in an airtight container to keep them soft and chewy. Enjoy with a glass of milk, a cup of tea, or simply on their own.

## Ranger Cookies

**Prep Time:** 15 mins
**Cooking Time:** 15 mins
**Yields:** 24 cookies

*Ingredients:*
1 cup (2 sticks) unsalted butter, softened
1 cup granulated sugar
1 cup packed light brown sugar
2 large eggs
1 teaspoon pure vanilla extract
2 cups all-purpose flour
1 teaspoon baking powder
1 teaspoon baking soda
1/2 teaspoon salt
2 cups rolled oats
1 cup shredded coconut
1 cup crispy rice cereal (e.g., Rice Krispies)
1 cup semisweet chocolate chips
1 cup chopped pecans or walnuts (optional)

*Directions:*
- Preheat your oven to 350°F (175°C). Line baking sheets with parchment paper or lightly grease them.
- In a large mixing bowl, cream together the softened butter, granulated sugar, and light brown sugar until the mixture is light and fluffy, which usually takes about 2-3 minutes.
- Add the eggs one at a time, beating well after each addition to ensure proper blending. Add the vanilla essence and stir.
- The all-purpose flour, baking soda, salt, and baking powder should be combined in a separate basin. Mixing until just incorporated, gradually add this dry mixture to the wet components.
- Gently fold in the rolled oats, shredded coconut, crispy rice cereal, semisweet chocolate chips, and chopped nuts (if using). The dough will become a delightful medley of textures.
- Using a tablespoon or cookie scoop, drop rounded tablespoons of cookie dough onto the prepared baking sheets. Leave enough space between each cookie to allow for spreading during baking.
- Bake in the preheated oven for 12-15 minutes, or until the cookies turn golden brown around the edges. The centres should still be slightly soft.
- Allow the Ranger Cookies to cool on the baking sheets for a few minutes before transferring them to wire racks to cool completely. Once cooled, these cookies are ready to transport you on a crunchy adventure in every bite.

# CHAPTER 2: SOUTH AMERICAN COOKIE SENSATIONS

## Alfajores from Argentina

**Prep Time:** 20 minutes
**Cook Time:** 10 minutes
**Yields:** 24 alfajores

### Ingredients:
1 cup (225g) unsalted butter, softened
1/2 cup (100g) granulated sugar
3 large egg yolks
1 teaspoon pure vanilla extract
2 cups (250g) all-purpose flour
1/2 cup (60g) cornstarch
1 teaspoon baking powder
1/4 teaspoon salt
Dulce de leche (caramel spread), for filling
Powdered sugar, for dusting

### Directions:
- In a large bowl, cream together the softened butter and granulated sugar until light and fluffy. This should take about 2-3 minutes.
- Combine the butter and sugar mixture with the egg yolks and vanilla essence. Combine well after mixing.
- Combine the all-purpose flour, cornstarch, baking soda, and salt in a separate basin.
- When a soft dough develops, gradually add the dry ingredient combination to the wet components while stirring. Just incorporate until the dough comes together without over-mixing.
- Make two equal parts of the dough. Make a disk out of each piece and wrap them in plastic wrap. To firm up the dough, place in the refrigerator for at least 30 minutes.
- Set a baking sheet on your oven's 350°F (175°C) rack and preheat the oven.
- Roll out one portion of the chilled dough on a lightly floured surface to about 1/4 inch thickness. Use a round cookie cutter to cut out cookies, then transfer them to the prepared baking sheet.
- Bake in the preheated oven for 8-10 minutes or until the edges of the cookies are just starting to turn golden. Be sure not to overbake; these cookies should remain pale.
- Take the cookies out of the oven and place them on a wire rack to cool.
- Once the cookies are completely cool, spread a generous layer of dulce de leche onto the bottom side of one cookie, and then sandwich it with another cookie, bottom sides together, creating a delightful alfajor.
- Dust the assembled alfajores with powdered sugar for a beautiful finishing touch.
- Allow the alfajores to set for about an hour before serving to allow the flavours to meld. They are best enjoyed with a cup of coffee or tea, or simply on their own.

## Cocadas Cookies

**Prep Time: 15 mins**
**Cooking Time: 20 mins**
**Yields: 24 cocadas**

*Ingredients:*
3 cups desiccated coconut
1 can (14 ounces) sweetened condensed milk
1/2 cup granulated sugar
1/4 cup water
1/4 teaspoon salt
1 teaspoon vanilla extract

*Directions:*
- Set your oven's temperature to 350°F (175°C). To keep things from sticking, line a baking sheet with parchment paper or gently oil it.
- Granulated sugar, water, and salt are combined in a pot over medium heat. Stirring is necessary until the sugar is completely dissolved and a little boil forms in the liquid. Simmer it for two to three minutes, or until it starts to thicken.
- In a large mixing bowl, combine the desiccated coconut and the sweetened condensed milk. Add the vanilla extract and mix well until the coconut is evenly coated with the milk.
- Gradually pour the hot sugar syrup into the coconut mixture, stirring continuously. Ensure that the syrup is well incorporated into the coconut mixture, creating a sticky, sweet mixture.
- Using a spoon or your hands, scoop out portions of the coconut mixture and shape them into small, compact rounds. Place these rounds onto the prepared baking sheet, spacing them about an inch apart.
- Place the baking sheet in the preheated oven and bake for approximately 18-20 minutes, or until the cocadas turn a beautiful golden brown colour and the edges begin to caramelise.
- Remove the cocadas from the oven and allow them to cool on the baking sheet for a few minutes. Place them on a wire rack to finish cooling. As they cool, the cocadas will firm up.
- Once completely cooled, your cocadas cookies are ready to enjoy. Savour the tropical flavours of toasted coconut and sweet caramelised goodness that transport you to the serene beaches of the Caribbean.

# South American Rosquillas

These charming, ring-shaped cookies are commonly found in Ecuador.

**Prep Time:** 20 mins
**Cooking Time:** 15 mins
Yields: 24 cookies

*Ingredients:*
2 cups all-purpose flour
1/2 teaspoon baking powder
1/4 teaspoon salt
1/2 cup unsalted butter, softened
1 cup granulated sugar
2 large eggs
1 teaspoon pure vanilla extract
Zest of one lemon (optional, for a citrusy twist)
Powdered sugar, for dusting (optional)

*Directions:*
- Set a baking sheet on your oven's 350°F (180°C) setting and prepare your oven.
- In a medium-sized bowl, sift together the all-purpose flour, baking powder, and salt. Set this dry mixture aside.
- In a separate large bowl, using an electric mixer or a wooden spoon, cream together the softened butter and granulated sugar until the mixture is light and fluffy. This should take about 2-3 minutes.
- Add the eggs one at a time, thoroughly blending between additions. Add the vanilla bean paste and, if using, the lemon zest. Your batter ought to be creamy and silky.
- Gradually add the dry mixture to the wet mixture, mixing until a soft dough forms. Be careful not to overmix; stop as soon as the ingredients are combined.
- Take a small portion of the dough (about 1 tablespoon) and roll it into a ball. Then, gently flatten it to create a round disc shape. You can also shape them into rings with a hole in the centre if you prefer a classic Rosquillas look.
- Place the shaped cookies onto the prepared baking sheet, leaving some space between each one. Bake in the preheated oven for approximately 12-15 minutes, or until the cookies are just beginning to turn golden around the edges.
- Take the cookies out of the oven and place them on a wire rack to cool. Once they've cooled completely, you can dust them with powdered sugar for a touch of sweetness and elegance.
- Your homemade South American Rosquillas Cookies are now ready to be enjoyed! Savour their delicate flavour with a cup of tea or share them with friends and family for a delightful treat that's sure to impress.

## Tortas Negras

These delightful treats are a cherished part of Colombian culture. These dark, dense cookies are akin to fruitcake cookies. They contain candied fruits, spices, and sometimes nuts, and are often enjoyed during holidays and celebrations.

**Prep Time: 20 mins**
**Cooking Time: 15 mins**
**Yields: 24 cookies**

### Ingredients:
2 cups all-purpose flour
1/2 cup panela or dark brown sugar
1/2 cup raisins
1/2 cup chopped candied fruit (such as figs, cherries, or citrus peel)
1/2 cup butter, softened
1/4 cup molasses
1/4 cup aguapanela (unrefined sugarcane juice) or dark corn syrup
1/4 cup brandy or dark rum (optional)
1 tsp ground cinnamon
1/2 tsp ground cloves
1/2 tsp ground nutmeg
1/2 tsp baking soda
1/4 tsp salt
Zest of one orange
Zest of one lemon
Powdered sugar for dusting (optional)

### Directions:
- Preheat your oven to 350°F (175°C). Line a baking sheet with parchment paper or grease it lightly.
- In a small bowl, combine the raisins and chopped candied fruit. If you're using brandy or dark rum, pour it over the fruit and let it soak while you prepare the rest of the ingredients. This will infuse the fruit with a delightful, boozy flavour.
- In a separate mixing bowl, whisk together the all-purpose flour, ground cinnamon, ground cloves, ground nutmeg, baking soda, and salt. Set this dry mixture aside.
- In a large mixing bowl, cream together the softened butter and panela (or dark brown sugar) until it becomes light and fluffy. This will take about 2-3 minutes.
- To the butter-sugar mixture, add the molasses, aguapanela (or dark corn syrup), orange zest, and lemon zest. Mix everything carefully until everything is incorporated.
- Add the dry flour mixture all at once to the wet ingredients. Mix until the dough comes together and there are no visible flour streaks.
- Drain the raisins and candied fruit if you soaked them in brandy or rum. Fold them into the cookie dough until evenly distributed.
- Take portions of the dough and roll them into small balls, approximately 1.5 inches in diameter. Place them on the prepared baking sheet, leaving a bit of space between each cookie as they will spread during baking.
- Bake the cookies in the preheated oven for 12 to 15 minutes, or until the edges are

golden brown. The middle of the cookies should still be a little mushy.

- Place the cookies on a wire rack to cool. If desired, dust them with powdered sugar for an extra touch of sweetness and decoration.

## Bolachas de Maizena

These delicate cornstarch cookies are popular in Brazil and Argentina. They are light, melt-in-your-mouth treats often filled with dulce de leche or jam. Bolachas de Maizena, also known as Maizena cookies. Their simplicity and melt-in-your-mouth texture make them a timeless classic.

**Prep Time: 15 mins**
**Cooking Time: 15 mins**
**Yields: 24 cookies**

### *Ingredients:*
Unsalted butter, 1 cup (225 grams), at room temperature
1 cup (125g) powdered sugar
2 cups (240g) cornstarch (Maizena)
1 cup (125g) all-purpose flour
1 teaspoon pure vanilla extract
1/2 teaspoon baking powder
Pinch of salt

### *Directions:*
- Set a baking sheet on your oven's 350°F (180°C) setting and prepare your oven.
- In a mixing bowl, cream the softened butter and powdered sugar together until light and fluffy. This process should take about 2-3 minutes, and it's essential for achieving the right texture in your cookies.
- Add the cornstarch (Maizena), all-purpose flour, baking powder, vanilla extract, and a pinch of salt to the butter-sugar mixture. Mix everything together until a smooth and cohesive dough forms. This should take about 2-3 minutes of gentle mixing.
- Roll the dough into small balls, each roughly the size of a walnut. Leave some space between the balls when you place them on the baking sheet that has been prepared. You can gently flatten each ball with the back of a fork, creating a classic crisscross pattern on top of each cookie.
- Bake the cookies in the preheated oven for 12-15 minutes or until they just start to turn golden around the edges. Be careful not to overbake them; Maizena cookies should remain pale in colour.
- Take the cookies out of the oven and let them cool for a few minutes on the baking sheet. They will be very delicate when hot, so handling them gently is crucial. After a brief cooling period, transfer the cookies to a wire rack to cool completely.
- Once the Bolachas de Maizena have cooled, they are ready to enjoy. These cookies have a wonderfully crumbly texture and a delicate, buttery flavour. They pair perfectly with a cup of tea or coffee or make a lovely treat for any occasion.

## Canestrelli

These intricate, flower-shaped cookies are a specialty in Uruguay. Canestrelli cookies are buttery and have a crumbly texture, often featuring a touch of lemon zest for flavour.

**Prep Time: 20 mins**
**Cooking Time: 12 mins**
**Yields: 30 cookies**

*Ingredients:*
1 cup (2 sticks) unsalted butter, softened
1/2 cup powdered sugar
2 large egg yolks
2 teaspoons pure vanilla extract
2 cups all-purpose flour
1/2 cup cornstarch
1/4 teaspoon salt
Zest of 1 lemon
Zest of 1 orange
Powdered sugar, for dusting

*Directions:*
- In a mixing dish, combine the powdered sugar and melted butter and beat until fluffy. It should take two to three minutes.
- To the butter-sugar mixture, include the egg yolks and vanilla extract. Mix until well combined.
- In a separate bowl, whisk together the all-purpose flour, cornstarch, and salt. Gradually add this dry mixture to the wet ingredients, mixing until a soft dough forms.
- Incorporate the lemon and orange zest into the dough, giving it a delightful citrus aroma and flavour. Mix until evenly distributed.
- Roll the dough into a ball, wrap it in plastic wrap, and refrigerate for at least 30 minutes. Chilling the dough will make it easier to handle.
- Set a baking sheet on your oven's 350°F (175°C) rack and preheat the oven.
- Take the chilled dough and pinch off small portions, rolling them into balls about the size of a walnut. Place the balls on the prepared baking sheet, leaving some space between each.
- Using the tines of a fork, gently press down on each cookie ball to create a crisscross pattern on the top. This not only adds a charming design but also helps the cookies bake evenly.
- Bake in the preheated oven for approximately 12 minutes or until the edges turn a light golden brown.
- Remove the Canestrelli cookies from the oven and let them cool on the baking sheet for a few minutes before transferring them to a wire rack to cool completely.
- Once the cookies have cooled, dust them generously with powdered sugar, adding a final touch of sweetness and a touch of elegance.
- Serve these delicate Canestrelli cookies with a cup of your favourite tea or coffee, and savour the buttery, citrusy goodness that

takes you straight to Italy with every bite. Enjoy!

## Brazilian Empanadas

While not strictly cookies, these small, hand-sized pastries are found in Brazil and are filled with a sweet or savoury filling, making them a delightful snack or dessert option.

**Prep Time: 30 mins**
**Cooking Time: 30 mins**
**Yields: 12 cookies**

*Ingredients:*
**For the Dough:**
2 cups all-purpose flour
1/2 cup unsalted butter, cold and cubed
1/2 teaspoon salt
1/4 cup cold water
1 egg yolk (for egg wash)

**For the Filling:**
1 cup cooked shredded chicken (or your choice of filling)
1/2 cup green olives, pitted and chopped
1/2 cup onions, finely chopped
2 cloves garlic, minced
1/2 cup cream cheese
1/2 cup grated Parmesan cheese
Salt and pepper to taste

*Directions:*
- Combine the flour and salt in a mixing dish.
- To the flour mixture, add the cold, diced butter. Work the butter into the flour with a pastry cutter or your hands until it resembles coarse crumbs.
- Mix in little amounts of cold water until the dough comes together. Don't overwork the dough, please.
- Divide the dough into two equal portions, wrap each in plastic wrap, and refrigerate for at least 30 minutes to chill.
- In a skillet over medium heat, sauté the onions and garlic until they become translucent.
- Add the shredded chicken (or your chosen filling) and cook until heated through.
- Stir in the green olives, cream cheese, and grated Parmesan cheese. Cook until the mixture is well combined and creamy.
- Season with salt and pepper to taste. Remove from the fire and let cool.
- Preheat your oven to 350°F (175°C) and grease a muffin tin.
- Roll out one portion of the chilled dough on a floured surface to about 1/4-inch thickness.
- Cut out circles from the dough using a cookie cutter or a glass that fits the muffin tin cups.
- Gently press each circle of dough into the greased muffin tin, forming a pastry shell.
- Fill each pastry shell with the prepared chicken and cheese mixture.
- Roll out the remaining dough portion and cut out circles for the top crusts.

- Place a dough circle on top of each filled pastry shell, and seal the edges by pressing them together with a fork.
- Whisk the egg yolk and brush it over the tops of the empadas for a golden finish.
- Bake in the preheated oven for about 25-30 minutes, or until the empadas are golden brown and crispy.
- Allow the Brazilian Empadas Cookies to cool slightly before removing them from the muffin tin.
- Serve them warm as a delightful snack or appetizer, and savor the flavors of Brazil in every bite.

## Hojarascas

Originating in Peru, hojarascas are thin, crumbly cookies often flavored with anise or cinnamon. They are typically dusted with powdered sugar and enjoyed during special occasions.

**Prep Time: 20 mins**
**Cooking Time: 15 mins**
**Yields: 24 cookies**

*Ingredients:*
2 cups all-purpose flour
1/2 cup powdered sugar
1/2 cup unsalted butter, softened
1/4 cup vegetable oil
1 teaspoon pure vanilla extract
1/2 teaspoon ground cinnamon
1/4 teaspoon ground cloves
1/4 teaspoon salt
Zest of one small lime (optional)
Powdered sugar, for dusting (optional)

*Directions:*
- Set a baking sheet on your oven's 350°F (175°C) rack and preheat the oven.
- Sift the all-purpose flour, powdered sugar, cinnamon, cloves, and salt together in a mixing basin. Add the zest of one tiny lime to the mixture if you want to give it a slight citrus flavor. To ensure the spices are distributed evenly, thoroughly mix.
- Cream the softened unsalted butter and vegetable oil until well blended in a another mixing bowl. The mixture ought to be smooth and creamy.
- Stir in the pure vanilla extract after adding it to the butter-oil combination.
- Add the dry ingredient combination to the wet components little by little. Use a spatula or your hands to combine everything until a soft, pliable dough forms.
- Pinch off small pieces of dough and roll them into balls, about the size of a walnut. Place the dough balls onto the prepared baking sheet, leaving some space between each one.
- Using a fork, gently press down on each cookie to flatten it slightly. Create a crisscross pattern on the top of each cookie for an authentic look and to help them bake evenly.
- Place the baking sheet in the preheated oven and bake for approximately 15 minutes, or until the cookies are golden

around the edges. Watch them carefully to prevent overbaking.
- Allow the Peruvian Hojarascas cookies to cool on a wire rack. Once they reach room temperature, dust them lightly with powdered sugar for an extra touch of sweetness.
- These delightful cookies are best enjoyed with a cup of hot Peruvian coffee or a soothing herbal tea. Share them with loved ones and savor the taste of Andean tradition.

## Sequilhos Cookies

Sequilhos Cookies are a beloved Brazilian treat that embodies the essence of simplicity and sweetness. These delightful, melt-in-your-mouth cookies are a true testament to the joy of uncomplicated pleasures. In this recipe, I'll guide you through the steps to create your own batch of these tender, crumbly delights, perfect for sharing with loved ones or savoring as a solo indulgence.

**Prep Time: 15 mins**
**Cooking Time: 20 mins**
**Yields: 24 cookies**

*Ingredients:*
2 cups of cornstarch
1 cup of granulated sugar
1/2 cup of unsalted butter, at room temperature
2 large eggs
1/2 teaspoon of baking powder
1/2 teaspoon of pure vanilla extract
A pinch of salt

*Directions:*
- Preheat your oven to 350°F (180°C) and line a baking sheet with parchment paper or a silicone baking mat.
- In a mixing bowl, cream together the room-temperature butter and granulated sugar until it's light and fluffy. This step is crucial for achieving that delightful melt-in-your-mouth texture, so take your time and ensure the mixture is well combined.
- Add the eggs one at a time, thoroughly blending between additions. This will help create a smooth, homogenous dough.
- Stir in the pure vanilla extract, incorporating it thoroughly into the mixture.
- In a separate bowl, sift the cornstarch, baking powder, and a pinch of salt together. This step ensures that there are no lumps in the dry ingredients.
- Gradually add the dry ingredients to the wet mixture. Mix gently but thoroughly until a soft, cohesive dough forms. The dough should be pliable and easy to work with.
- Using your hands, roll small portions of the dough into 1-inch (2.5 cm) balls and place them on the prepared baking sheet. You can lightly grease your hands with a touch of butter to prevent sticking.
- Flatten each dough ball slightly with a fork, creating a crisscross pattern on the

surface. This not only adds a lovely visual touch but also helps the cookies bake evenly.
- Bake the cookies in the preheated oven for approximately 20 minutes or until they turn a pale golden color around the edges. Keep a close eye on them, as their delicate nature means they can easily overbake.
- After baking, take the cookies out of the oven and let them cool for a while on the baking sheet. They will be fragile when hot, so handle them gently.
- After a brief cooling period, transfer the Sequilhos Cookies to a wire rack to cool completely. They will continue to firm up as they cool, achieving that sought-after crumbly texture.
- Serve and enjoy! These cookies are perfect with a cup of coffee or tea, or simply on their own as a sweet, satisfying treat.

## Brazilian Brigadeiros Cookies

Brazilian Brigadeiros are beloved treats in Brazil, cherished at celebrations and gatherings. These delightful chocolate fudge-like confections have been reimagined as cookies in this recipe. These cookies are sure to become a favorite at any occasion.

**Prep Time: 20 mins**
**Cooking Time: 10 mins**
**Yields: 24 cookies**

*Ingredients:*
1/2 cup unsalted butter, softened
1 cup sweetened condensed milk
2 tablespoons cocoa powder
2 cups chocolate cookie crumbs (from chocolate wafers or chocolate sandwich cookies)
1 cup chocolate sprinkles (jimmies) for coating
1/4 teaspoon salt

*Directions:*
**Prepare Cookie Dough:**
- In a mixing bowl, combine the softened butter and sweetened condensed milk. Mix until well incorporated.
Gradually add the cocoa powder to the mixture, stirring continuously until the cocoa is fully integrated and the dough becomes smooth.
Add Cookie Crumbs:
- Fold in the chocolate cookie crumbs and a pinch of salt into the dough. Mix until everything comes together, forming a uniform, slightly sticky dough.

**Shape the Cookies:**
- Scoop out tiny amounts of dough and roll them into 2.5-cm (1-inch) balls. You can lightly grease your hands with butter to prevent sticking.
- Roll each ball in chocolate sprinkles until fully coated, giving them a delightful texture and appearance.

**Chill the Cookies:**
- Place the Brigadeiros cookies on a baking sheet lined with parchment paper or a silicone baking mat.

- Refrigerate the cookies for at least 20 minutes or until they firm up.

**Serve and Enjoy:**
- Once the cookies have chilled, they are ready to be savored. Watch them vanish as you serve them up on a dish.

**Storage:** Brigadeiros cookies can be kept at room temperature for up to three days in an airtight container. Refrigerate for up to a week if you need extended storage.

## Peruvian Polvorones Cookies

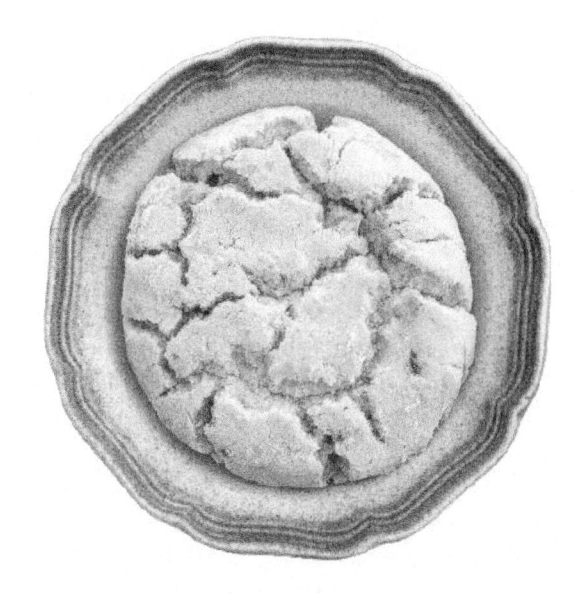

Peruvian Polvorones are a delightful treat that captures the essence of Peru's rich culinary heritage. These melt-in-your-mouth cookies are a perfect blend of delicate shortbread and sweet dulce de leche. Whether enjoyed with a cup of coffee or as an elegant dessert, Peruvian Polvorones are sure to transport you to the heart of Peru with every bite.

**Prep Time:** 30 minutes
**Cooking Time:** 12 minutes
**Yields:** 24 cookies

*Ingredients:*
**For the Cookie Dough:**
1 cup (2 sticks) unsalted butter, softened
1/2 cup powdered sugar
1 teaspoon pure vanilla extract
2 cups all-purpose flour
1/2 cup cornstarch
A pinch of salt

**For the Filling and Coating:**
1 cup dulce de leche, either handmade or purchased
Sugary granules for dusting

The oven should be preheated at 350°F (180°C). Use parchment paper to line a baking sheet or gently oil it.
- The softened butter and powdered sugar should be combined in a large mixing basin and creamed until light and fluffy. It could take three to four minutes.
- Add the vanilla essence and stir. Combine the flour, cornstarch, and a dash of salt in a separate basin. Mix until the dough comes together, then gradually add the dry mixture to the butter mixture. Watch out not to combine too much.
- Make one-inch balls out of little amounts of the dough. Place the cookies on the prepared baking sheet, spacing them apart. Each cookie should be lightly flattened using the back of a fork to make a crisscross pattern.
- The cookies should be baked in the preheated oven for 12 minutes or until the edges are lightly brown. The tops should

still be a delicate color. As they cool, they will continue to firm up, so avoid overbaking.
- After the cookies have finished cooling on the baking sheet for a few minutes, move them to a wire rack to finish cooling. They are delicate when warm, so handle them with care.
- Once the cookies have cooled completely, spread a generous amount of dulce de leche on the flat side of one cookie and then sandwich it with another cookie, creating a "sandwich." Repeat this process with the remaining cookies.
- Finally, dust the assembled Peruvian Polvorones with powdered sugar for a lovely finishing touch. You can use a fine-mesh sieve to achieve an even, delicate dusting.
- Your Peruvian Polvorones Cookies are now ready to be savored. Serve them with a cup of tea or coffee, and delight in the sweet flavors of Peru.

## Colombian Arequipe Thumbprint Cookies

Colombian Arequipe Thumbprint Cookies are a delightful blend of rich, buttery cookies and luscious arequipe, a sweet caramel-like spread loved by Colombians and South Americans alike. These cookies are a tribute to the sweet tooth that runs deep in Colombian culture. They make for a perfect treat to enjoy with a cup of coffee or as an indulgent dessert.

**Prep Time: 15 mins**
**Cooking Time: 15 mins**
**Yields: 24 cookies**

*Ingredients:*
1 cup unsalted butter, softened
1/2 cup granulated sugar
2 large egg yolks
2 teaspoons pure vanilla extract
2 cups all-purpose flour
1/4 teaspoon salt
1/2 cup arequipe (Colombian caramel spread)
1/4 cup finely chopped toasted almonds (optional, for garnish)

*Directions:*
- Set a baking sheet on your oven's 350°F (175°C) rack and preheat the oven.
- The softened butter and granulated sugar should be combined in a large mixing basin and creamed until light and fluffy. It ought should take two to three minutes.
- The egg yolks and vanilla essence should be well mixed together.
- Mix the salt and all-purpose flour in a another basin. The dough will come together if you gradually add this dry component to the butter mixture while mixing. Just blend until there are no longer any flour streaks, being careful not to overmix.
- Make one-inch balls out of little amounts of the dough. Place these on the prepared baking sheet, leaving about 2 inches of space between each cookie.

- Gently press your thumb or the back of a teaspoon into the center of each cookie ball, creating a well or indentation.
- Spoon a small amount of arequipe into each thumbprint, filling it just below the rim.
- Place the cookies in the preheated oven and bake for 12-15 minutes, or until the edges turn lightly golden.
- If desired, while the cookies are still warm, sprinkle finely chopped toasted almonds over the arequipe filling for an extra layer of flavor and crunch.
- After the cookies have cooled slightly on the baking sheet, move them to a wire rack to finish cooling. As they cool, the arequipe will set, creating a deliciously gooey center.

# CHAPTER 3: EUROPEAN COOKIE ELEGANCE

## French Macarons with Various Fillings

French Macarons, with their delicate, crispy shells and luscious fillings, are the epitome of elegance in the world of cookies. These bite-sized beauties have captured hearts around the globe, from the bustling streets of Paris to home kitchens everywhere.

**Prep Time: 30 mins**
**Cooking Time: 15 mins**
**Yields: 24 filled macarons**

*Ingredients:*
**For the Macaron Shells:**
1 cup (100g) almond flour
1 3/4 cups (210g) confectioners' sugar
3 large egg whites, at room temperature
1/4 cup (50g) granulated sugar
A pinch of cream of tartar (optional)
Gel food coloring (optional)
1/2 teaspoon vanilla extract (optional)
**For the Fillings:**
Ganache (dark chocolate, white chocolate, or flavored ganache of your choice)
Fruit preserves (such as raspberry, strawberry, or passion fruit)
Buttercream (various flavors like vanilla, chocolate, or pistachio)
Nutella or other hazelnut spreads
Lemon or orange curd
Salted caramel sauce
Whipped cream with fresh berries

*Directions:*
- **Sift and Combine Dry Ingredients:** In a bowl, sift together the almond flour and confectioners' sugar. This step is crucial for a smooth macaron shell.
- **Whip Egg Whites:** In a separate clean, dry bowl, beat the room-temperature egg whites until they become foamy. Add a pinch of cream of tartar (if using) to help stabilize the meringue.

Gradually add granulated sugar while continuing to whip. Whip until you achieve stiff, glossy peaks. Optionally, add gel food coloring and vanilla extract at this stage.

- **Fold Dry Ingredients:** Gently fold the sifted dry ingredients into the egg white mixture. Be cautious not to deflate the meringue; this should result in a smooth, thick batter with a ribbon-like consistency.
- **Pipe Macaron Shells:** Transfer the batter to a piping bag fitted with a round tip (typically a 1/2 inch tip). Pipe small rounds (about 1.5 inches in diameter) onto parchment paper or a silicone baking mat, spacing them at least an inch apart to allow for spreading. Tap the baking sheet firmly on the counter to release any air bubbles, and let the piped macarons rest for 30 minutes to develop a smooth, glossy surface.
- **Bake:** Preheat your oven to 300°F (150°C). Bake the macarons for 12-15 minutes, or until they have formed "feet" (ruffled edges) and are set but not browned. Depending on your oven, the baking time may change.
- **Cool and Fill:** Let the macarons cool completely on the baking sheet. Once cooled, gently peel them off the parchment paper or mat.
- **Assemble:** Pair up macaron shells of similar sizes. Fill one shell with your choice of filling (ganache, buttercream, preserves, etc.), then sandwich it with another shell.
- **Rest and Enjoy:** Allow the filled macarons to rest in an airtight container in the refrigerator for at least 24 hours before serving. This resting time allows the flavors to meld and the texture to mature.

## Italian Amaretti Cookies

Italian Amaretti Cookies are a delightful confection that captures the essence of Italy's culinary artistry. These gluten-free almond cookies boast a delicate, crisp exterior that gives way to a chewy, almond-infused center. Perfect for any occasion, they are a sweet taste of Italy you can enjoy with a cup of espresso or as an elegant dessert.

**Prep Time: 20 mins**
**Cooking Time: 18 mins**
**Yields: 24 cookies**

*Ingredients:*
2 cups almond flour
1 cup granulated sugar
2 large egg whites, room temperature
1 teaspoon almond extract
1/4 teaspoon pure vanilla extract
A pinch of salt
Powdered sugar, for dusting (optional)

*Directions:*
- Set a baking sheet on your oven's 325°F (160°C) setting and preheat it.
- Almond flour, sugar, and a dash of salt are mixed together in a large basin. These dry

components should be thoroughly combined.
- The egg whites should be whisked until they form soft peaks in a separate bowl. You may do this by hand or with a hand mixer, but for best results, make sure the bowl and beaters are clean and dry.
- Create a fragrant, velvety concoction by gently incorporating the almond and vanilla extracts into the beaten egg whites.
- Add the combination of dry ingredients gradually to the egg white mixture. They should be folded until a smooth, sticky dough comes together. It must be substantial enough to maintain its form.
- Roll the dough into little, uniformly sized balls with your hands that are approximately 1 inch in diameter. To help shaping the cookies easier, briefly moisten your hands or lightly dusted them with almond flour if the dough is too sticky.
- Arrange the cookie balls on the baking sheet that has been prepared, allowing room between each one.
- Using your fingertips, gently press each biscuit into a disc form. The tops of the cookies can optionally be dusted with powdered sugar for a beautiful presentation.
- Bake the cookies for 15 to 18 minutes, or until they have a light golden color and a crisp exterior, in the preheated oven. Even though they will stiffen up as they cool, the center will still be mushy.
- Take the cookies out of the oven and let them cool for a few minutes on the baking sheet before transferring them to a wire rack to finish cooling.
- Once cooled, store the Italian Amaretti Cookies in an airtight container. They can be enjoyed immediately or over the course of a few days. These cookies also make wonderful gifts for loved ones who appreciate the taste of Italy.

## German Lebkuchen Cookies

German Lebkuchen cookies, often referred to as gingerbread cookies, are a beloved treat during the festive holiday season in Germany and beyond. These spiced and honey-sweetened cookies are a delightful blend of warmth and comfort, perfect for enjoying with a cup of mulled wine or hot cocoa.

**Prep Time: 30 mins**
**Cooking Time: 15 mins**
**Yields: 24 cookies**

*Ingredients:*
2 cups all-purpose flour
1/2 cup ground almonds
1/2 cup granulated sugar
1/2 cup honey
1/4 cup molasses

1/4 cup unsalted butter
1 large egg
1 tablespoon Lebkuchen spice mix (a blend of cinnamon, cloves, allspice, and nutmeg)
1 teaspoon baking powder
1/2 teaspoon baking soda
1/4 teaspoon salt
Zest of one lemon
Zest of one orange
1/2 cup candied citrus peel, chopped
1/2 cup blanched almonds, whole or slivered
1/2 cup powdered sugar (for icing)

*Directions:*
- **Prepare the Dough:** In a medium-sized saucepan, combine the honey, molasses, and butter over low heat. Stir until the butter has melted, and the mixture is well combined. As soon as it reaches room temperature, remove from the heat.
- **Mix the Dry Ingredients:** In a large mixing bowl, whisk together the flour, ground almonds, sugar, Lebkuchen spice mix, baking powder, baking soda, and salt.
- **Combine Wet and Dry Ingredients:** Once the honey and butter mixture has cooled, add it to the dry ingredients along with the egg, lemon zest, and orange zest. Mix until a smooth dough forms.
- **Fold in Candied Citrus and Almonds:** Gently fold in the chopped candied citrus peel and almonds until they are evenly distributed throughout the dough.
- **Chill the Dough:** Wrap the dough in plastic wrap and refrigerate it for at least 2 hours or overnight. Chilling the dough will make it easier to handle and shape.
- **Preheat Your Oven:** Preheat your oven to 350°F (175°C) and line baking sheets with parchment paper.
- **Shape the Cookies:** On a lightly floured surface, roll out the dough to about 1/4-inch thickness. Cut out the shapes you choose using cookie cutters.
- **Bake the Cookies:** Place the cookies on the prepared baking sheets and bake for 12-15 minutes, or until they are golden brown around the edges.
- **Cool and Ice:** Allow the cookies to cool on a wire rack. Once they are completely cooled, mix the powdered sugar with a little water to make a thick icing. Drizzle or pipe the icing over the cookies for a decorative touch.
- **Enjoy:** Your homemade German Lebkuchen cookies are ready to be enjoyed! Serve them with a warm beverage and savor the rich, spiced flavors of the holiday season.

## Spanish Almond Tuiles

Spanish Almond Tuiles are a true testament to the elegance and simplicity of Spanish cuisine. These delicate, lace-like cookies are known for their crisp texture and rich almond flavor. They're the perfect accompaniment to a cup of coffee or a scoop of ice cream, and they'll transport you straight to the sun-drenched streets of Spain with every bite.

**Prep Time: 15 mins**
**Cooking Time: 10 mins**
**Yields: 24 tuiles**

*Ingredients:*
1/2 cup (115g) unsalted butter, melted
1/2 cup (100g) granulated sugar
2 large egg whites
1 teaspoon almond extract
1/2 cup (60g) all-purpose flour
1/4 cup (25g) finely chopped almonds
Pinch of salt

*Directions:*
- Set a baking sheet on your oven's 350°F (175°C) rack and preheat the oven.
- The melted butter and granulated sugar should be well mixed in a mixing dish. Add the egg whites and almond extract, then mix until the batter is smooth.
- Gently fold in the all-purpose flour, finely chopped almonds, and a pinch of salt. The resulting batter should have a smooth consistency.
- Drop small spoonfuls of the batter onto the prepared baking sheet, spacing them about 3 inches apart. Use the back of a spoon to spread each spoonful into a thin, circular shape. Keep in mind that the cookies will spread during baking, so leave ample space between them.
- Place the baking sheet in the preheated oven and bake for about 8 to 10 minutes, or until the edges of the tuiles turn a golden brown color. Keep a close eye on them as they can quickly go from golden to over-baked.
- As soon as the tuiles come out of the oven, they'll be pliable. Working quickly, use a thin spatula to lift each tuile and gently shape it into a curved or folded form. You can drape them over a rolling pin or the edge of a cup to create a curved shape.
- Allow the shaped tuiles to cool completely on a wire rack. Once cooled, they'll become wonderfully crisp and delicate. Serve them as a delightful snack or alongside your favorite dessert.

## Russian Tea Cakes

Russian Tea Cakes, also known as Mexican Wedding Cookies or Snowball Cookies, are beloved for their melt-in-your-mouth texture and delicate sweetness. These delightful little treats are perfect for any occasion, whether you're sharing them at a festive gathering or enjoying a quiet afternoon tea. With just a handful of ingredients and a dash of love, you can create these powdered sugar-coated gems that are sure to bring smiles to the faces of those lucky enough to taste them.

**Prep Time: 20 minutes**
**Cooking Time: 12-15 minutes**
**Yields: 36 cookies**

*Ingredients:*
1 cup unsalted butter, softened
1/2 cup powdered sugar, plus extra for coating
1 teaspoon pure vanilla extract
2 1/4 cups all-purpose flour
1/4 teaspoon salt
1 cup finely chopped nuts (walnuts or pecans work well)

*Directions:*
- **Preheat Your Oven:** Begin by preheating your oven to 350°F (175°C). For simple cleanup, cover a baking sheet with parchment paper.
- **Cream the Butter:** Place the softened butter in a large mixing bowl and beat it until it is creamy and fluffy. You may either do this by hand with a wooden spoon or with a hand mixer.
- Add sugar and vanilla extract: Add the pure vanilla essence and 1/2 cup of powdered sugar gradually. Mix the dough on and off until it is thoroughly incorporated and just barely creamy.
- Mix the dry ingredients in: Mix the salt and all-purpose flour in a another basin. To the butter and sugar mixture, gradually add this dry ingredients. Mix until the dough comes together and no longer has any visible flour streaks.
- Gently incorporate chopped nuts: Add your preferred nuts, which have been finely chopped. It is customary to use walnuts or pecans, but you are welcome to substitute your preferred kind.
- To shape the cookies, divide the dough into tiny sections and form each into a 1-inch ball. These balls should be spaced approximately an inch apart on the baking sheet you have prepared. During baking, these cookies won't spread too much.
- **Bake to Perfection:** Bake the cookies in your preheated oven for approximately 12-15 minutes, or until they just start to turn a light golden brown. Be careful not to overbake them; they should remain pale.
- **Roll in Powdered Sugar:** While the cookies are still warm but not hot, gently roll each one in powdered sugar until they're evenly coated. This will create that iconic "snowball" appearance.
- **Cool and Re-Coat:** Allow the cookies to cool completely on a wire rack. Once cooled, give them another roll in powdered sugar for that extra snowy finish.
- **Enjoy:** Serve these Russian Tea Cakes on a decorative platter, share them with friends, or savor them with a hot cup of tea or coffee. These delicate delights are sure to impress.

## Italian Biscotti:

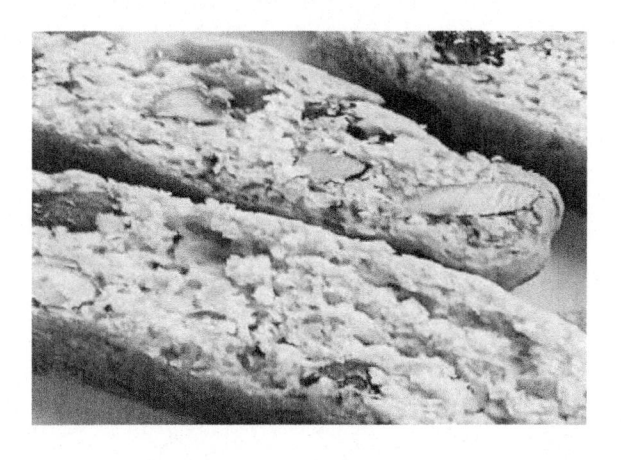

Twice-baked Italian cookies that are perfect for dipping in coffee or wine. They come in various flavors, including almond, anise, and chocolate. In this recipe, we'll unlock the secrets to crafting these delightful treats that pair perfectly with a cup of espresso or a glass of Vin Santo.

**Prep Time: 15 mins**
**Cooking Time: 45 mins**
**Yields: 24 biscotti**

*Ingredients:*
2 cups all-purpose flour
1 cup granulated sugar
2 teaspoons baking powder
1/2 teaspoon salt
3 large eggs
1 teaspoon pure vanilla extract
1/2 cup almonds, toasted and coarsely chopped
1/2 cup dried cranberries or your choice of dried fruits

*Directions:*
- **Preheat and Prepare:** - Prepare by preheating the oven to 350°F (175°C). Use silicone baking mats or parchment paper to line a baking pan.
- **Combine by ingredients:** Combine the dry ingredients by whisking the all-purpose flour, salt, sugar, and baking powder together in a large mixing basin.
- **Mix Wet Ingredients:** In a separate bowl, whisk the eggs and vanilla extract until frothy.
- **Incorporate Wet into Dry:** Pour the egg mixture into the dry ingredients and stir until a dough forms. It may seem crumbly at first, but continue to mix until it comes together.
- **Fold in Add-Ins:** Gently fold in the toasted chopped almonds and dried cranberries (or your choice of dried fruits). The dough should be slightly sticky.
- **Shape the Dough:** Divide the dough in half. With lightly floured hands, shape each portion into a log approximately 12 inches long and 2 inches wide. On the baking sheet that has been prepared, arrange the logs with room between them.
- First Bake: Bake the logs in the preheated oven for approximately 25 minutes, or until they are firm to the touch and golden brown.
- Slightly Cool: Take the biscotti logs out of the oven and let them cool for approximately 10 minutes on the baking sheet. Lower the oven's setting to 325°F (160°C).
- **Slice the Biscotti:** Using a sharp knife, slice the logs diagonally into 1/2-inch wide pieces. Arrange the biscotti on the baking sheet, cut sides up.
- **Second Bake:** Return the biscotti to the oven and bake for an additional 15-20 minutes, or until they are crisp and lightly golden. Flip them over halfway through this second baking time for even toasting.
- **Cool Completely:** Remove the biscotti from the oven and allow them to cool completely on a wire rack. They will become even crisper as they cool.
- **Enjoy:** Serve your homemade Italian biscotti with a hot beverage of your choice, and savor the satisfying crunch and subtle sweetness that make these cookies a beloved Italian classic.

# Linzer Cookies:

Linzer cookies are a delightful Austrian and German classic, known for their elegant appearance and irresistible flavor. These delicate sandwich cookies are a true work of art, with their latticework tops and vibrant raspberry jam centers. Perfect for special occasions or afternoon tea, Linzer cookies are a sweet ode to European craftsmanship and tradition.

**Prep Time: 30 mins**
**Cooking Time: 15 mins**
**Yields: 24 Linzer cookies**

*Ingredients:*
**For the Cookie Dough:**
Unsalted butter, 1 cup (2 sticks), at room temperature
1/2 cup granulated sugar
1 large egg
1 teaspoon pure vanilla extract
2 cups all-purpose flour
1 cup finely ground almonds
1/2 teaspoon ground cinnamon
Zest of one lemon
1/4 teaspoon salt

**For Assembly and Filling:**
1/2 cup raspberry jam (or any preferred fruit jam)
Confectioners' sugar, for dusting

*Directions:*
- **Prepare the Dough:** In a large mixing bowl, cream together the softened butter and granulated sugar until light and fluffy. Add the egg and vanilla extract, continuing to mix until well combined.
- **Combine the Dry Ingredients:** In a separate bowl, whisk together the flour, ground almonds, ground cinnamon, lemon zest, and salt.
- **Incorporate Dry Ingredients:** Gradually add the dry ingredient mixture to the wet ingredients, mixing until a soft dough forms. Be careful not to overmix; just combine until the dough comes together.
- **Chill the Dough:** Separate the dough into two equal pieces, and then form each piece into a disk.
  Wrap them in plastic wrap and refrigerate for at least 1 hour, or until the dough is firm and easy to handle.
- **Preheat the Oven:** Preheat your oven to 350°F (180°C) and line baking sheets with parchment paper.
- **Roll and Cut:** On a lightly floured surface, roll out one of the dough disks to a 1/8-inch thickness. Use a Linzer cookie cutter to cut out rounds. For half of the rounds, use a smaller shape cutter to create a center cutout. Place these on the prepared baking sheets.
- **Bake the Cookies:** Bake the cookies in the preheated oven for 12-15 minutes or until they turn a light golden brown. Allow them

to cool on the baking sheets for a few minutes before transferring them to a wire rack to cool completely.

- **Assemble the Cookies:** Spread a small amount of raspberry jam onto the solid cookie rounds, leaving the center cutout cookies plain.

- **Create the Sandwiches:** Place a cookie with a cutout on top of each jam-covered cookie to create the iconic Linzer sandwich. Gently press them together.

- **Dust with Confectioners' Sugar:** Finally, dust the top of each Linzer cookie with confectioners' sugar for a beautiful finishing touch.

## Speculoos (Belgium/Netherlands)

Speculoos, a beloved cookie hailing from the heart of Europe, brings warm and spicy flavors to your palate. Originating in Belgium and the Netherlands, these thin, crisp cookies are often enjoyed with a cup of coffee or tea. Their distinctive blend of cinnamon, nutmeg, and cloves will transport you to the cozy streets of Brussels or Amsterdam with each delightful bite.

**Prep Time: 20 mins**

**Cooking Time: 15 mins**
**Yields: 24 cookies**

*Ingredients:*

1 1/2 cups all-purpose flour
1/2 cup unsalted butter, softened
1/2 cup brown sugar, packed
1/4 cup granulated sugar
1 egg
1 teaspoon ground cinnamon
1/2 teaspoon ground nutmeg
1/4 teaspoon ground cloves
1/4 teaspoon baking powder
1/4 teaspoon salt

*Directions:*

- In a mixing bowl, sift together the all-purpose flour, ground cinnamon, ground nutmeg, ground cloves, baking powder, and salt. Set aside.
- In a separate bowl, cream together the softened unsalted butter, brown sugar, and granulated sugar until the mixture is light and fluffy. This should take about 2-3 minutes.
- Stir the egg well into the butter-sugar mixture after adding it.
- As you gradually combine the dry and liquid components, a nice cookie dough will develop.
- Make two equal amounts of the cookie dough, and then flatten each portion into a disk. Refrigerate them for at least 30 minutes after wrapping them in plastic wrap. The dough may be handled and rolled out more easily after being chilled.
- Set a baking sheet on your oven's 350°F (175°C) rack and preheat the oven.
- One of the refrigerated dough disks should be rolled out to a thickness of about 1/8 inch

on a floured board. To make different forms, you may use cookie cutters, or you can just use a knife to cut it into squares.
- On the prepared baking sheet, arrange the cut-out cookies, allowing space between them.
- Bake for 12 to 15 minutes, or until the edges of the cookies are golden brown, in the preheated oven. Keep an eye on them because your oven's baking times may differ.
- When the cookies are finished baking, take them out of the oven and let them cool on a wire rack. As they cool, they will continue to solidify.
- Roll and bake the second disk of dough as you did with the first until all of your Speculoos cookies are done and ready to eat.

## Italian Pizzelle

Pizzelle, delicate and beautifully patterned Italian waffle cookies, have been a cherished treat in Italy for generations. These wafer-thin delights are known not only for their intricate designs but also for their irresistible flavor. Let's embark on a journey to Italy and discover the art of making Pizzelle.

**Prep Time: 15 mins**
**Cooking Time: 30 mins**

**Yields: 24 pizzelle**

*Ingredients:*
2 cups all-purpose flour
1 1/2 teaspoons baking powder
3/4 cup granulated sugar
3 large eggs
1/2 cup unsalted butter, melted and cooled
1 teaspoon pure vanilla extract
A pinch of anise seeds (optional, for flavor)

*Directions:*
- **Preheat the Pizzelle Maker:** Plug in your pizzelle maker and allow it to preheat according to the manufacturer's instructions. It should reach the desired temperature before you start cooking.
- **Prepare the Batter:** In a medium-sized bowl, whisk together the flour and baking powder. In a separate larger bowl, beat the eggs and sugar together until the mixture becomes smooth and slightly pale in color.
- **Combine Wet and Dry Ingredients:** Gradually add the melted butter, vanilla extract, and anise seeds (if using) to the egg and sugar mixture. Mix until well combined.
- **Make the Pizzelle:** Gently fold the dry ingredients into the wet ingredients until you have a smooth batter. While still spreadingable, the batter should be thick. If it's too thick, you can add a small amount of milk to achieve the desired consistency.
- **Bake the Pizzelle:** Lightly grease the pizzelle maker with a small amount of cooking spray or a brush of melted butter. Place a heaping tablespoon of batter onto the center of each patterned circle on the pizzelle maker. Close the lid and cook according to the manufacturer's instructions,

usually for about 30-45 seconds, or until the pizzelle are golden brown.

- **Remove and Cool:** Carefully remove the pizzelle from the maker using a spatula or tongs. Put them on a wire rack to finish cooling. As they cool, they will become crisp.

- **Serve and Enjoy:** Pizzelle can be enjoyed as-is or shaped while warm into cones, cylinders, or bowls to hold ice cream or other fillings. Dust with powdered sugar or drizzle with melted chocolate for extra indulgence.

## French Palmiers

Palmiers, also known as elephant ears or palm leaves, are a classic French pastry that captivates with its simplicity and elegance. These golden, flaky delights are made from just two ingredients yet manage to capture the essence of French patisserie. In this section, we'll guide you through the process of creating these delicious treats, allowing you to bring a taste of France into your own kitchen.

**Prep Time: 15 minutes**

**Cooking Time: 15 minutes**
**Yields: 24 palmiers**

*Ingredients:*
1 sheet of handmade or store-bought puff pastry
1 cup granulated sugar

*Directions:*
- **Preheat the Oven:** Begin by preheating your oven to 400°F (200°C). Ensure the oven is well heated before you start baking to achieve that perfect flakiness.

- **Prepare the Sugar:** Spread a generous amount of granulated sugar evenly over a clean work surface. You can use a rolling pin to help even it out.

- **Roll Out the Puff Pastry:** Lay out your sheet of puff pastry on top of the sugar. Press it down gently to help the sugar adhere to the pastry.

- **Fold the Sides:** Starting with one long edge of the pastry, carefully fold it inward towards the center, stopping at the middle. Repeat the process with the opposite edge, creating a double fold that meets in the center of the pastry sheet.

- **Final Fold and Chill:** Fold the pastry in half along the centerline, creating a book-like shape. Gently press it together. Wrap the pastry in plastic wrap and place it in the freezer for about 10 minutes to firm up slightly.

- **Slice into Palmiers:** Remove the pastry from the freezer and slice it into approximately 1/2-inch thick pieces using a sharp knife. Lay the slices on a baking sheet lined with parchment paper, leaving some space between each.

- **Bake to Golden Perfection:** Bake the palmiers in the preheated oven for about 12-15 minutes or until they turn a beautiful golden brown. Keep an eye on them as baking times may vary depending on your oven.
- **Cool and Serve:** Once baked, remove the palmiers from the oven and allow them to cool on a wire rack. As they cool, they'll crisp up, revealing their delightful flakiness.
- **Enjoy:** Serve your freshly baked palmiers with a hot cup of coffee or tea and savor the taste of France in each delicate, sugary bite.

## Norwegian Krumkake Cookie

Krumkake, hailing from the enchanting land of Norway, is a cherished Norwegian cookie that embodies the essence of delicate, crisp perfection. With its intricate pattern and rich history, Krumkake captures the heart and soul of Norwegian baking. Join me on this delightful journey as we explore the art of crafting these thin, beautifully rolled waffle-like cookies that will transport your taste buds to the picturesque fjords of Scandinavia.

**Prep: 15 mins**
**Cooking Time: 20 mins**

**Yields: 24 Krumkake**

*Ingredients:*
1 cup all-purpose flour
1/2 cup granulated sugar
2 large eggs
1/2 cup unsalted butter, melted
1/2 cup whole milk
1/2 teaspoon pure vanilla extract
1/4 teaspoon ground cardamom (optional, for a traditional Norwegian flavor)
Pinch of salt

*Directions:*
- **Preheat and Prepare:** Preheat your Krumkake iron or Pizzelle maker according to the manufacturer's instructions. Ensure it's well-greased to prevent sticking.
- **Mix Dry Ingredients:** In a mixing bowl, whisk together the all-purpose flour and ground cardamom (if using). Set this mixture aside.
- **Whisk Wet Ingredients:** In a separate bowl, whisk the granulated sugar and eggs together until they become pale and creamy. This should take about 2-3 minutes.
- **Combine Wet and Dry:** Gradually add the melted butter, whole milk, pure vanilla extract, and a pinch of salt to the egg and sugar mixture. Continue to whisk until well combined.
- **Create Batter:** Slowly incorporate the dry ingredients into the wet mixture. Whisk until a smooth batter forms. The batter should resemble thick cream in consistency.
- **Bake the Krumkake:** Place a spoonful of batter onto the preheated Krumkake iron. Close the iron and cook until the cookies are golden brown and have a delicate lace-like

pattern, usually about 20-30 seconds, depending on your iron.

- **Shape the Krumkake:** Quickly remove the delicate Krumkake using a spatula or a Krumkake roller. While the cookie is still hot, gently roll it around a wooden or metal cone-shaped Krumkake roller to give it its classic cylindrical shape. Hold it in place for a few seconds to set the shape, and then transfer it to a wire rack to cool completely. Apply the remaining batter in a similar manner.

- **Serve and Enjoy:** Once the Krumkake has cooled and become crispy, it's ready to be enjoyed. You can leave them plain or fill them with whipped cream, fruit preserves, or Nutella for an extra indulgence.

# CHAPTER 4: ASIAN COOKIE EXTRAVAGANZA

## Chinese Almond Cookies

Chinese Almond Cookies are a beloved treat in Chinese-American cuisine, and their delicate, nutty flavor and crisp texture make them a delightful addition to any cookie platter. These cookies have a fascinating history, often associated with celebrations and symbolism in Chinese culture. In this recipe, we'll show you how to recreate this timeless favorite in your own kitchen.

**Prep Time: 15 mins**
**Cooking Time: 15 mins**
**Yields: 24 cookies**

*Ingredients:*
1 cup (2 sticks) unsalted butter, softened
1 cup granulated sugar
1 large egg
1 teaspoon almond extract
2 1/2 cups all-purpose flour
1/2 cup finely ground almond meal
1/2 teaspoon baking powder
1/2 teaspoon salt
24 whole blanched almonds, for garnish
Egg wash (1 egg beaten with 1 tablespoon water), for brushing

*Directions:*
- Preheat your oven to 350°F (175°C). Use silicone baking mats or parchment paper to line two baking sheets.
- In a large mixing basin, combine the softened butter and sugar and beat until fluffy. Normally, this takes two to three minutes.
- Beat the butter-sugar mixture well after adding the egg and almond extract.
- Combine the all-purpose flour, almond meal, baking powder, and salt in a separate basin.
- As you gradually combine the dry and liquid components, a soft dough will begin to form. Avoid over-mixing, and stop as soon as the dough comes together.
- Using a cookie scoop or a spoon, divide the dough into pieces, and then roll each portion into a 1-inch ball. Place the dough balls on the preheated baking sheets with a

distance of around 2 inches between each one.
- Using your thumb or the back of a teaspoon, gently press down in the center of each cookie to create an indentation. Place a blanched almond in the center of each indentation.
- Brush the top of each cookie with the egg wash, which gives them a beautiful golden sheen when baked.
- Bake in the preheated oven for 12-15 minutes, or until the cookies' edges turn golden brown.
- Remove the cookies from the oven and allow them to cool on the baking sheets for a few minutes before transferring them to a wire rack to cool completely.

## Japanese Matcha Shortbread

This delicate treat is a fusion of the rich cultural heritage of Japan and the simple pleasures of buttery, crumbly shortbread. With a harmonious balance of earthy matcha and sweet butter, these cookies offer a taste of Zen-like serenity with each bite.

**Prep: 20 mins**
**Cooking Time: 15 mins**
**Yields: 24 cookies**

*Ingredients:*
1 cup (2 sticks) unsalted butter, softened
1/2 cup powdered sugar
2 cups all-purpose flour
2 tablespoons high-quality matcha powder
1/4 teaspoon salt
1 teaspoon vanilla extract (optional, for added flavor)

*Directions:*
- **Preheat the Oven:** Set your oven's temperature to 350°F (175°C). To keep things from sticking, line a baking sheet with parchment paper or gently oil it.
- **Cream the Butter and Sugar:** In a mixing bowl, cream together the softened unsalted butter and powdered sugar until the mixture is light and fluffy. You can use a hand mixer or mix by hand using a wooden spoon.
- **Sift the Dry Ingredients:** In a separate bowl, sift together the all-purpose flour, matcha powder, and salt. Sifting will help ensure an even distribution of matcha and prevent lumps.
- **Combine the Ingredients:** Gradually add the sifted dry ingredients to the creamed butter and sugar mixture. Mix until a crumbly dough forms. If desired, add the vanilla extract at this stage for an extra layer of flavor.
- **Shape the Shortbread:** Turn the dough out onto a clean surface or a piece of parchment paper. Gently knead it until it comes together, being careful not to overwork the dough. Form it into a log shape, about 2 inches in diameter.
- **Chill the Dough:** Wrap the dough log in plastic wrap and refrigerate it for at least 30 minutes. Chilling the dough will make it

easier to slice and maintain its shape during baking.

- **Slice and Bake:** Once the dough is firm, remove it from the refrigerator and unwrap it. Using a sharp knife, slice the dough into 1/4-inch thick rounds. Place the rounds on the prepared baking sheet, leaving a little space between each cookie.
- **Bake to Perfection:** Bake the matcha shortbread in the preheated oven for 12 to 15 minutes or until the edges turn lightly golden. Keep a close eye on them, as matcha can brown quickly.
- **Cool and Enjoy:** Let the cookies cool for a few minutes on the baking sheet, then move them to a wire rack to finish cooling. As it cools, the shortbread will solidify.
- **Serve with Serenity:** Once cooled, savor the subtle bitterness of matcha combined with the buttery goodness of shortbread. These cookies are perfect for a moment of Zen-inspired indulgence, whether enjoyed with a cup of green tea or as a delightful snack on their own.

## Indian Nan Khatai

Indian Nan Khatai is a delightful and melt-in-your-mouth shortbread cookie that hails from the vibrant culinary heritage of India. These aromatic and delicately spiced cookies are known for their crumbly texture and the perfect balance of sweetness and warmth. In this recipe, we'll guide you through the process of creating these heavenly treats in the comfort of your own kitchen.

**Prep Time: 15 mins**
**Cooking Time: 15 mins**
**Yields: 24 cookies**

*Ingredients:*
1 cup (2 sticks) unsalted butter, softened
1 cup all-purpose flour
1/2 cup chickpea flour (besan)
1 cup powdered sugar
1/4 teaspoon cardamom powder
1/4 teaspoon baking powder
A pinch of salt
Chopped pistachios or almonds for garnish (optional)

*Directions:*
- **Preheat the Oven:** Set your oven to 350°F (175°C) before using it. Use parchment paper to line a baking sheet or gently oil it.
- **Sift the dry ingredients:** Combine the all-purpose flour, chickpea flour, baking powder, cardamom powder, and a dash of salt in a mixing bowl. The flours are nicely mixed and aerated thanks to sifting.
- **Cream Butter and Sugar:** In a separate dish, combine the softened butter and powdered sugar and beat until well-combined. It ought should take two to three minutes.
- **Combine Wet and Dry Ingredients:** Add the dry ingredients, which have been sifted, gradually to the butter-sugar mixture. Mix until a soft, malleable dough forms.
 Be careful not to overmix; just combine the ingredients until they come together.
- **Shape the Cookies:** Take small portions of the dough and shape them into small balls.

Place them on the prepared baking sheet, leaving some space between each cookie. You can flatten them slightly with the back of a fork or your fingers for a traditional Nan Khatai appearance.

- **Garnish:** If desired, press a chopped pistachio or almond into the center of each cookie for a decorative touch.
- **Bake:** Place the baking sheet in the preheated oven and bake for approximately 15 minutes or until the edges of the cookies turn golden brown. Keep a close eye on them as baking times may vary slightly based on your oven.

**Cool and Serve:** Once baked, remove the cookies from the oven and allow them to cool on the baking sheet for a few minutes. After that, move them to a wire rack to finish cooling. Indian Nan Khatai is best enjoyed with a cup of hot tea or coffee.

## Thai Mango Sticky Rice Cookies

Inspired by the beloved Thai dessert, Khao Niew Mamuang, these cookies capture the perfect blend of sweet mango, creamy coconut, and fragrant sticky rice. They're a delightful fusion of tradition and innovation that will leave you craving more.

**Prep Time: 30 mins**
**Cooking Time: 15 mins**

**Yields: 24 cookies**

*Ingredients:*
**For the Cookie Dough:**
1 cup unsalted butter, softened
1/2 cup granulated sugar
1/4 cup sweetened condensed milk
2 cups all-purpose flour
1/2 cup glutinous (sticky) rice flour
1/4 teaspoon salt
1/2 teaspoon vanilla extract

**For the Filling:**
1 ripe mango, diced into small pieces
1/2 cup coconut cream
1/4 cup granulated sugar
A pinch of salt

*Directions:*
- **Prepare the Mango Filling:** In a small saucepan, combine the diced mango, coconut cream, granulated sugar, and a pinch of salt. Cook over medium-low heat, stirring occasionally, until the mixture thickens and the mango is soft and tender. This should take about 10-12 minutes.
Remove from heat and let the mango filling cool to room temperature.

- **Make the Cookie Dough:** In a large mixing bowl, cream together the softened butter and granulated sugar until light and fluffy. Add the sweetened condensed milk and vanilla extract, continuing to mix until well combined.

- **Combine Dry Ingredients:** In a separate bowl, whisk together the all-purpose flour, glutinous rice flour, and salt.

- **Mix the Dough:** Gradually add the dry ingredients to the butter mixture, mixing until a smooth cookie dough forms.

- **Assemble the Cookies:** Take a small portion of the cookie dough (about a tablespoon), flatten it in your palm, and place a teaspoon of the mango filling in the center. Fold the edges of the dough over the filling, sealing it to form a ball. Gently flatten it to create a cookie shape. For the remaining dough and filling, repeat this procedure.
- **Bake the Cookies:** Preheat your oven to 350°F (175°C).

Place the formed cookies on a baking sheet lined with parchment paper, leaving some space between them. Bake in the preheated oven for 12-15 minutes or until the edges turn golden brown.

- **Cool and Enjoy:** Once baked, allow the cookies to cool on a wire rack for a few minutes.

Serve your Thai Mango Sticky Rice Cookies with a cup of tea or coffee and savor the delightful blend of flavors.

## Filipino Polvorón

**Prep Time: 20 mins**
**Cooking Time: 20 mins**
**Yields: 12 polvorón**

*Ingredients:*
1 cup all-purpose flour
1 cup powdered milk
1/2 cup granulated sugar
1/2 cup unsalted butter, melted
1/2 cup toasted rice flour
1/4 cup crushed toasted pinipig (toasted glutinous rice)

*Directions:*
- In a pan over medium heat, toast the rice flour until it turns golden brown, stirring constantly to prevent burning. This should take about 5-7 minutes. Set aside to cool.
- In a large mixing bowl, combine the all-purpose flour and powdered milk. They should be well combined to prevent lumps.
- In a separate bowl, melt the unsalted butter in the microwave or on the stovetop. Allow it to cool slightly.
- Pour the melted butter into the flour and powdered milk mixture. Mix thoroughly until it forms a crumbly texture.
- Add the granulated sugar and toasted rice flour to the mixture. Mixing should continue until all components are well incorporated.
- Gently fold in the crushed toasted pinipig, adding a delightful crunch to the polvorón mixture.
- Prepare a polvorón molder or you can use your hands. Scoop a portion of the mixture into the molder, press it down firmly, and release it onto a tray lined with wax paper or parchment paper. Repeat this process for the remaining mixture.
- Allow the polvorón to set at room temperature for about 2 hours or until they become firm.

- Once the polvorón have set, wrap them individually in colorful cellophane or wax paper, twisting the ends to secure them.
- Your homemade Filipino Polvorón is now ready to enjoy. Serve them as sweet treats for dessert or snack time, and savor the delightful flavors of the Philippines in each bite.

## Korean Yakgwa

Yakgwa, a traditional Korean honey flower cookie, embodies the essence of Korean cuisine with its delicate balance of sweetness and subtle floral undertones. These golden, flower-shaped treats are a cherished part of Korean culture, often enjoyed during special occasions and celebrations. In this recipe, we will guide you through the process of creating these fragrant and indulgent sweets, bringing a taste of Korea to your kitchen.

**Prep Time: 20 mins**
**Cooking Time: 20 mins**
**Yields: 20 cookies**

**Ingredients:**
1 cup all-purpose flour
1/4 cup rice flour
1/4 cup honey
1/4 cup sesame oil
1/4 cup sugar
1/4 cup water
1/4 teaspoon salt
Cooking oil (for frying)
Toasted sesame seeds (for garnish)
Optional: pine nuts or slivered almonds for decoration

***Directions*:**
- **Prepare the Dough:** In a mixing bowl, combine the all-purpose flour and rice flour. Stir them together until well-mixed. In a separate saucepan, mix the honey, sesame oil, sugar, and water. Heat this mixture over low heat, stirring constantly until the sugar is completely dissolved. It should be taken off the stove and given some time to cool. Gradually add the honey mixture to the flour mixture, stirring continuously. Keep mixing until the dough forms. It should be soft and pliable. If it's too dry, add a little more water; if too sticky, add a bit more flour.
- **Shape the Yakgwa:** Lightly dust your work surface with flour. Roll the dough into a thin sheet, about 1/4 inch thick. Use a flower-shaped cookie cutter or any desired shape to cut out the cookies. If you don't have cookie cutters, you can use a knife to cut them into diamond or rectangle shapes. Optionally, place a pine nut or slivered almond in the center of each cookie for decoration.
- **Fry the Cookies:** In a deep frying pan or a small saucepan, heat cooking oil over medium heat. To check if the oil is hot enough, you can drop a small piece of dough into the oil; if it sizzles and rises to the surface, the oil is ready. Carefully place the shaped cookies into the hot oil, a few at a time. Fry them until they turn golden brown and crisp, flipping them occasionally to ensure even cooking. Once fried, remove the

cookies from the oil and place them on a paper towel-lined plate to absorb excess oil.
- **Garnish and Serve:** While the cookies are still warm, lightly brush them with honey for a glossy finish. Sprinkle toasted sesame seeds over the cookies for added flavor and texture. Before serving, let the cookies cool fully. As they cool, they will get sharper.

## Indonesian Kue Lidah Kucing

Indonesian Kue Lidah Kucing, also known as Cat's Tongue Cookies, are a beloved treat in Indonesia. These delicate, crisp, and buttery cookies get their name from their resemblance to cat's tongues. They are often enjoyed with a cup of tea or coffee and make for a delightful snack or dessert.

**Prep Time: 20 mins**
**Cooking Time: 12 mins per batch**
**Yields: 45 cookies**

*Ingredients:*
100 grams (about 1/2 cup) unsalted butter, softened
100 grams (about 3/4 cup) powdered sugar
2 egg whites
1/4 teaspoon vanilla extract
100 grams (about 3/4 cup) all-purpose flour
A pinch of salt

*Directions:*
- **Preheat Your Oven:** Preheat your oven to 180°C (350°F) and line a baking sheet with parchment paper.
- **Cream Butter and Sugar:** In a mixing bowl, cream the softened butter and powdered sugar together until the mixture becomes light and fluffy. You can use an electric mixer or beat by hand.
- **Add Egg Whites:** Gradually add the egg whites to the butter-sugar mixture, one at a time, mixing well after each addition. Beat the mixture continuously until it is well-combined and smooth.
- **Salt and Vanilla essence:** Add a dash of salt and a few drops of vanilla essence. These will improve the cookies' taste.
- **Gently fold in the flour:** Once you have a smooth mixture, fold in the all-purpose flour. Just blend until there are no longer any flour streaks, being careful not to overmix.
- **Pipe the Batter:** Spoon the cookie batter into a piping bag with a tiny round tip (about 1/4 inch in diameter). If you don't have a piping bag, you can use a plastic bag that has had a little corner cut off that can be resealed.
- **Pipe Cat's Tongue Shapes:** On the prepared baking sheet, pipe small, finger-length lines of the cookie batter, leaving some space between each one. These will resemble the shape of cat's tongues.
- **Bake:** Place the baking sheet in the preheated oven and bake for 10-12 minutes or until the edges of the cookies turn golden brown.

- **Cool:** Once done, remove the cookies from the oven and allow them to cool on the baking sheet for a few minutes. As they cool, they will get firmer.
- **Serve:** Your Indonesian Kue Lidah Kucing, Cat's Tongue Cookies, are ready to enjoy! Serve them with a cup of tea or coffee and savor their delicate, buttery goodness.

## Taiwanese Pineaple Cakes

Taiwanese Pineapple Cakes are a beloved and iconic treat in Taiwan, known for their delicate pastry and sweet pineapple filling. These delightful cakes are often enjoyed during special occasions and make for perfect gifts.

**Prep Time: 45 mins**
**Cooking Time: 20 mins**
**Yields: 16 pineapple cakes**

*Ingredients:*
**For the Pineapple Filling:**
2 cups of fresh pineapple, finely chopped and drained
1/2 cup of granulated sugar
1/4 cup of maltose (or honey as a substitute)
2 tablespoons of butter
1/4 teaspoon of salt
1/4 teaspoon of pineapple extract (optional, for enhanced flavor)

**For the Pastry:**
2 cups of all-purpose flour
1/2 cup of unsalted butter, cold and cubed
1/4 cup of powdered sugar
2 egg yolks
2 tablespoons of milk
1/4 teaspoon of salt
1/4 teaspoon of baking powder

*Directions:*
**Making the Pineapple Filling:**
- In a saucepan, combine the finely chopped pineapple, granulated sugar, and maltose (or honey) over medium heat.
- Stir the mixture frequently until it thickens and turns into a jam-like consistency. This should take about 20-25 minutes.
- Add the butter, salt, and pineapple extract (if using) to the pineapple jam. Continue to cook and stir until the mixture is smooth and glossy.
- Remove the pineapple filling from the heat and allow it to cool completely. Once cooled, shape it into small, 1-inch diameter balls and set aside.

**Preparing the Pastry:**
- In a mixing bowl, combine the cold, cubed butter and powdered sugar. Use a pastry cutter or your fingertips to work the butter into the sugar until it resembles coarse crumbs.
- Add the egg yolks and milk to the mixture, and gently mix until it forms a soft, pliable dough.
- In a separate bowl, sift together the all-purpose flour, salt, and baking powder.

- Gradually add the dry ingredients to the dough, mixing until everything is well incorporated. Create a smooth ball out of the dough.

Preheat the oven to 350°F (180°C) and prepare a baking sheet with parchment paper before putting the pineapple cakes together.

- Divide the pastry dough into small, equal portions, and flatten each portion into a round disc.
- Place a pineapple filling ball in the center of each pastry disc and wrap the dough around it, sealing the edges. Gently shape them into small, rectangular cakes.
- Place the assembled pineapple cakes on the prepared baking sheet, leaving some space between each cake.
- Bake in the preheated oven for about 15-20 minutes or until the cakes turn golden brown.

**Final Steps:**

- Remove the Taiwanese Pineapple Cakes from the oven and allow them to cool on a wire rack.
- Once completely cooled, store the cakes in an airtight container. They are best enjoyed after a day or two when the flavors have melded together.

# Vietnamese Sesame Peanut Candy (Keo Me Phung)

Vietnamese Sesame Peanut Candy, known as "Keo Me Phung," is a delightful and crunchy confectionery that's popular in Vietnamese cuisine. This sweet treat combines the nutty goodness of roasted peanuts with the fragrant, toasty flavors of sesame seeds, all bound together by a luscious caramel. Keo Me Phung is not only a beloved snack but also a lovely gift to share with friends and family.

**Prep Time: 15 mins**
**Cooking Time: 15 mins**
**Yields: 20 pieces**

*Ingredients:*

1 cup roasted unsalted peanuts
1/2 cup white sesame seeds
1 cup granulated sugar
1/2 cup water
1/4 teaspoon salt
1/4 teaspoon vanilla extract (optional)

*Directions:*

- **Prepare the Peanuts and Sesame Seeds:** Coarsely chop the roasted peanuts, leaving some whole for texture. Toast the white sesame seeds in a dry pan over low heat until they turn golden brown and release their aroma. Be sure to keep them moving to prevent burning. Once toasted, set aside.

- **Make the Caramel:** In a saucepan over medium heat, combine the granulated sugar and water. Stir until the sugar has dissolved. Continue to cook the sugar mixture, without stirring, until it turns a deep amber color. This may take about 10-12 minutes. Watch it closely to prevent burning. Swirl the pan gently if needed to ensure even caramelization.

- **Add Peanuts and Sesame Seeds:** Once the caramel reaches the desired color, remove the saucepan from the heat immediately. Quickly stir in the roasted peanuts and toasted sesame seeds. Work swiftly but carefully as the caramel will be very hot. If desired, add a pinch of salt and vanilla extract for extra flavor. Mix well to ensure the nuts and seeds are evenly coated with caramel.

- **Shape the Candy:** Prepare a baking sheet lined with parchment paper or a silicone baking mat.

Using a greased spoon or your hands (be cautious as the mixture is hot), scoop out small portions of the caramel-nut mixture and place them on the prepared baking sheet. You can shape them into rounds or squares, depending on your preference.

- **Cool and Serve:** Allow the candies to cool and harden for about 30 minutes to 1 hour. They will become crisp as they cool. Once completely cooled and set, gently remove the candies from the parchment paper or baking mat. Store the Vietnamese Sesame Peanut Candy in an airtight container at room temperature. They make delightful snacks and homemade gifts for special occasions.

## Malaysian Kuih Bangkit

Malaysian Kuih Bangkit is a delightful, traditional Malaysian cookie that's known for its delicate, melt-in-your-mouth texture and subtle pandan and coconut flavors. These bite-sized cookies are a favorite during festive occasions like Chinese New Year and Hari Raya Aidilfitri. Making Kuih Bangkit at home is a wonderful way to connect with Malaysian culture and enjoy a sweet treat that's beloved by many.

**Prep Time: 20 mins**
**Cooking Time: 15 mins**
**Yields: 50-60 cookies**

*Ingredients:*
250g of tapioca flour
60g of cornstarch
150g of icing sugar
2 pandan leaves (for pandan juice)
2 egg yolks
100ml of coconut milk
A pinch of salt
Red food coloring (optional)
Banana leaves or parchment paper for lining the baking tray

*Directions:*
- **Prepare Pandan Juice:** Wash and cut the pandan leaves into small pieces.
Blend the pandan leaves with a little water to create a smooth pandan juice.
Strain the juice through a fine sieve or cheesecloth to extract the green liquid. Set aside.
- **Mix Dry Ingredients:** In a large mixing bowl, sift together the tapioca flour and cornstarch. Add the icing sugar and a pinch of salt, and mix well.
- **Combine Wet Ingredients:** In a separate bowl, whisk the egg yolks and coconut milk together until well combined. Gradually add the pandan juice to the egg yolk and coconut milk mixture, stirring until you achieve a vibrant green color. You can add a few drops of red food coloring to enhance the color if desired.
- **Form the Dough:** Make a well in the center of the dry ingredients. Gradually pour the wet ingredients mixture into the well while stirring continuously until a soft dough forms. If the dough is too sticky, you can add a little more tapioca flour until it's easy to handle.
- **Shape the Cookies:** Take small portions of the dough and roll them into small balls or shape them using traditional Kuih Bangkit molds for intricate patterns.
Place the shaped cookies onto a baking tray lined with banana leaves or parchment paper, leaving a small gap between each cookie.
- **Bake:** Preheat your oven to 150°C (300°F).
Bake the cookies in the preheated oven for about 15 minutes or until they turn a pale golden color. Be careful not to overbake, as Kuih Bangkit should remain light in color.
- Cool and Store: Allow the cookies to cool on the baking tray for a few minutes before transferring them to a wire rack to cool completely. Once fully cooled, store your Malaysian Kuih Bangkit in an airtight container to maintain their delicate texture and flavors.

## Japanese Dorayaki

Dorayaki, a beloved Japanese sweet, is a delightful confection that consists of fluffy pancake-like layers sandwiched together with a luscious filling, traditionally sweet red bean paste. This treat is not only visually charming but also incredibly delicious, making it a favorite among both children and adults. In this recipe, we'll guide you through the steps to create your own batch of homemade Japanese Dorayaki, so you can savor the authentic flavors of Japan from the comfort of your own kitchen.

**Prep Time: 15 mins**
**Cooking Time: 15 mins**
**Yields: 6 Dorayaki**

*Ingredients:*
1 cup all-purpose flour
1 teaspoon baking powder
2 large eggs
1/2 cup granulated sugar

1 tablespoon honey
1 teaspoon pure vanilla extract
2 tablespoons water
1/4 cup red bean paste (store-bought or homemade)

*Directions:*

- **Sift and Combine Dry Ingredients:** In a mixing bowl, sift together 1 cup of all-purpose flour and 1 teaspoon of baking powder. They should be well combined to prevent lumps.
- **Whisk the Eggs:** In a separate bowl, whisk 2 large eggs until they are well-beaten and slightly frothy.
- **Add Sugar and Honey:** Gradually add 1/2 cup of granulated sugar and 1 tablespoon of honey to the beaten eggs. Continue to whisk until the mixture becomes smooth and the sugar is fully dissolved.
- **Incorporate Vanilla Extract:** Stir in 1 teaspoon of pure vanilla extract to the egg mixture.
- **Combine Wet and Dry Ingredients:** Gently fold the sifted dry ingredients into the egg mixture. Be careful not to overmix; just blend until the batter is smooth.
- **Adjust Consistency:** If the batter is too thick, add 2 tablespoons of water and mix until the batter reaches a slightly runny consistency. This will help create light and fluffy Dorayaki pancakes.
- **Heat the Pan:** Preheat a non-stick skillet or griddle over medium-low heat. You can lightly grease the surface with a small amount of vegetable oil, but it's not necessary if you're using a non-stick pan.
- **Cook the Pancakes:** Pour about 1/4 cup of the batter onto the heated skillet to form a round pancake. Cook until you see bubbles forming on the surface, then flip the pancake and cook the other side until it's golden brown. This should take approximately 1-2 minutes per side. Repeat this step for the remaining batter, making sure to maintain a consistent size for each pancake.
- **Cool and Fill:** Allow the pancakes to cool completely. Once they have cooled, spread a generous tablespoon of red bean paste onto the center of one pancake, then top it with another to create a Dorayaki sandwich.
- **Serve and Enjoy:** Your homemade Dorayaki is ready to be enjoyed! Serve them at room temperature and savor the delightful combination of soft, sweet pancakes and the earthy sweetness of red bean paste.

## Chinese Mooncakes

Chinese Mooncakes are more than just a treat; they are a symbol of tradition, family, and festivity. These round pastries, often filled with sweet or savory fillings, play a central role in celebrating the Mid-Autumn Festival, a time when family and friends gather to admire the full moon and exchange well-wishes. In this recipe, we'll guide you through the art of crafting these delectable delights, allowing you to partake in this cherished Chinese tradition.

**Prep Time: 30 mins**

**Cooking Time:** 25 mins
**Yields:** 12 mooncakes

*Ingredients:*
For the Dough:
250 grams of all-purpose flour
40 grams of golden syrup
40 grams of vegetable oil
A pinch of salt
1/2 teaspoon of lye water (optional, for color and texture)
**For the Filling (Red Bean Paste):**
300 grams of sweet red bean paste (store-bought or homemade)
2 tablespoons of vegetable oil
**For the Egg Wash:**
1 egg yolk
1 teaspoon of water
**For the Decorative Patterns (Optional):**
Mooncake molds with your preferred design

*Directions:*
- **Prepare the Filling:** If using store-bought red bean paste, skip to step 2. For homemade red bean paste, cook red beans until soft, mash them, and cook with sugar until a thick, smooth paste forms. Stir in vegetable oil and let it cool.
- **Make the Dough:** In a mixing bowl, combine all-purpose flour, golden syrup, vegetable oil, a pinch of salt, and lye water (if using).
Mix the ingredients until they come together to form a smooth dough. If it's too dry, add a bit more water; if too sticky, add a bit more flour.
The dough has to be smooth and malleable after a few minutes of kneading.
- **Divide Dough and Filling:** Divide the dough into smaller portions, each about 25 grams, and the red bean paste into portions of 30 grams.
- **Assemble the Mooncakes:** Flatten a piece of dough into a small disk. Place a portion of red bean paste in the center. Wrap the dough around the filling, ensuring it's completely sealed. Roll it into a ball and gently flatten it.
- **Decorate the Mooncakes (Optional):** If you have mooncake molds, dust them with a little flour and press the assembled mooncakes into the molds to create decorative patterns.
- **Prepare the Egg Wash:** In a small bowl, whisk the egg yolk with a teaspoon of water to create the egg wash.
- **Bake the Mooncakes:** Preheat your oven to 350°F (180°C). Place the assembled mooncakes on a baking tray lined with parchment paper. Brush the mooncakes with a thin layer of the egg wash.
- **Baking:** Bake the mooncakes for about 10 minutes. Remove from the oven, let them cool for 10 minutes, and brush with a second layer of egg wash.
- **Second Baking:** Return the mooncakes to the oven and bake for another 15 minutes or until they turn golden brown.
- **Cool and Store:** Allow the mooncakes to cool completely on a wire rack before storing them in an airtight container.

# CHAPTER 5: AFRICAN COOKIE ADVENTURES

## Moroccan Almond Crescents

Indulge in the exotic flavors of North Africa with these Moroccan Almond Crescents. These crescent-shaped cookies are a delightful blend of nutty almond flavors, aromatic spices, and a dusting of powdered sugar. Perfect for sipping with a cup of mint tea or sharing with friends and family, these cookies bring a taste of Morocco right to your kitchen.

**Prep Time: 20 mins**
**Cooking Time: 15 mins**
**Yields: 24 crescent cookies**

*Ingredients:*
1 cup almond meal
1 cup all-purpose flour
1/2 cup unsalted butter, softened
1/4 cup powdered sugar, plus extra for dusting
1/4 teaspoon ground cinnamon
1/4 teaspoon ground cardamom
1/4 teaspoon vanilla extract
Pinch of salt

*Directions:*
- **Pre-heat the Oven:** Set your oven to 350 degrees Fahrenheit (175 degrees Celsius) and line a baking sheet with parchment paper.
- **Prepare the Dough:** In a mixing bowl, combine the softened butter and powdered sugar. Beat together until creamy and smooth.
- **Add the Almond Meal:** Gradually add the almond meal to the butter mixture, blending well until fully incorporated.
- **Sift and Add Dry Ingredients:** Sift the all-purpose flour, ground cinnamon, ground cardamom, and a pinch of salt into the bowl. Add the vanilla extract as well. Mix until the dough comes together. It should be soft and slightly sticky.
- **Shape the Crescents:** Take a small portion of the dough and roll it between your palms to form a small log. Then, shape it into a crescent shape by bending the log slightly. Place the crescent-shaped cookies on the prepared baking sheet, leaving a bit of space between each one.
- **Bake:** Place the baking sheet in the preheated oven and bake for about 15 minutes, or until the edges of the crescents turn a light golden brown.
- **Cool and Dust:** Remove the Moroccan Almond Crescents from the oven and allow them to cool on a wire rack for a few minutes. While they are still warm, dust the tops generously with powdered sugar.

- **Serve:** Once completely cooled and the powdered sugar has set, your Moroccan Almond Crescents are ready to be enjoyed. Serve them alongside a cup of hot tea or coffee for the perfect Moroccan treat.

## South African Hertzog Cookies

South Africa, with its breathtaking landscapes and diverse cultures, offers a delightful array of flavors in its cuisine. Among its many culinary treasures, South African Hertzog Cookies stand out as a true taste of sunshine. These sweet and tangy treats are named after General J.B.M. Hertzog, a former South African Prime Minister, and they capture the warmth and zest of this beautiful country. Let's embark on a journey to make these delightful cookies that are sure to brighten your day.

**Prep Time: 20 mins**
**Cooking Time: 15 mins**
**Yields: 24 cookies**

*Ingredients:*
2 cups all-purpose flour
1 cup desiccated coconut
1 cup granulated sugar
2 large eggs
2 tablespoons smooth apricot jam
2 tablespoons unsalted butter, melted
1 teaspoon baking powder
1/2 teaspoon salt
Zest of 1 lemon
1 tablespoon fresh lemon juice

*Directions:*
- **Preheat and Prepare:** Preheat your oven to 350°F (175°C) and line a baking sheet with parchment paper or lightly grease it.
- **Mix Dry Ingredients:** In a large mixing bowl, combine the all-purpose flour, desiccated coconut, granulated sugar, baking powder, and salt. These dry components should be well mixed.
- Add Wet Ingredients: Lightly whisk the eggs in a separate basin. Add the smooth apricot jam, lemon juice, lemon zest, and melted butter after that. Stir vigorously to fully combine the wet ingredients.
Combining the wet and dry ingredients will result in a soft dough. Add the wet mixture gradually while stirring gently with a spatula or wooden spoon. Avoid overmixing; the dough should only just come together.
- **Shape the Cookies:** Take small portions of the dough and roll them into balls, approximately 1 inch in diameter. Place these balls on the prepared baking sheet, leaving some space between each one.
- **Make an Indentation:** Use your thumb or the back of a teaspoon to create a small indentation in the center of each cookie. This is where you'll add the apricot jam filling.
- **Fill with Jam:** Spoon a small amount of smooth apricot jam into the indentation of each cookie. Be generous but avoid overfilling to prevent the jam from overflowing during baking.
- **Bake:** Place the baking sheet in the preheated oven and bake for about 15 minutes or until the cookies turn a light golden brown. Keep a close eye on them to avoid overcooking.

- **Cool and Enjoy:** When the cookies are finished baking, take them out of the oven and let them cool on a wire rack. The jam-filled centers will set as the cookies cool. Once completely cooled, indulge in the sweet and tangy goodness of South African Hertzog Cookies.

## Egyptian Basbousa Cookies

Egyptian Basbousa cookies are a delightful Middle Eastern treat that captures the essence of the region's sweet traditions. These moist, semolina-based cookies are drenched in fragrant rosewater and orange blossom syrup, offering a harmonious balance of textures and flavors. Perfect for celebrations or as a sweet ending to any meal, Basbousa cookies are a beloved treat across Egypt and beyond.

**Prep Time: 20 mins**
**Cooking Time: 30 mins**
**Yields: 24 cookies**

*Ingredients:*
For the Basbousa:
2 cups fine semolina
1 cup plain yogurt
1 cup granulated sugar
1/2 cup unsalted butter, melted
1/4 cup desiccated coconut
1/4 cup blanched almonds, for garnish
1 teaspoon baking powder
1/2 teaspoon vanilla extract
Zest of 1 lemon
**For the Syrup:**
1 1/2 cups granulated sugar
1 1/2 cups water
1 tablespoon rosewater
1 tablespoon orange blossom water
Juice of 1/2 lemon

**Directions:**
- **Preheat the Oven:** Preheat your oven to 350°F (180°C) and grease a 9x13-inch (23x33 cm) baking dish or an equivalent-sized rectangular baking pan.
- **Prepare the Basbousa Batter:** In a large mixing bowl, combine the semolina, sugar, desiccated coconut, baking powder, and lemon zest. Mix well to combine.
- **Add Wet Ingredients:** Pour in the melted butter, plain yogurt, and vanilla extract into the dry ingredients. Mix thoroughly until a smooth batter forms. Let it rest for 10 minutes to allow the semolina to absorb the moisture.
- **Transfer to Baking Dish:** Pour the Basbousa batter into the greased baking dish, spreading it evenly with a spatula. Smooth the surface.
- **Cut into Diamond Shapes:** Using a sharp knife, lightly score the surface of the Basbousa batter into diamond or square shapes. Each piece should have a blanched almond in the middle.
- **Bake:** Put the baking dish in the preheated oven, and bake it for approximately 30 minutes, or until the Basbousa turns golden brown and a toothpick inserted in the center comes out clean.

- To make the syrup, mix sugar and water in a pot while the basbousa bakes. After bringing it to a boil, turn the heat down, and let it simmer for ten minutes. Add the rosewater, orange blossom water, and lemon juice by stirring. Take it off the fire and let it a minute to cool.
- **Soak the Basbousa:** As soon as the Basbousa comes out of the oven, pour the warm syrup evenly over the hot cookies. Ensure that the syrup soaks into the cuts you made earlier.
- **Cool and Serve:** Allow the Basbousa to cool completely in the pan, absorbing the aromatic syrup. Once cooled, cut along the scored lines, and serve these delectable Egyptian Basbousa cookies to enjoy a taste of the Middle East.

## Nigerian Chin-Chin

Nigerian Chin-Chin cookies are a beloved West African treat that holds a special place in the hearts of many. These delightful, bite-sized cookies are crispy on the outside and slightly soft on the inside, offering a wonderful contrast of textures. Seasoned with a hint of nutmeg and a touch of sweetness, Chin-Chin cookies are perfect for snacking, sharing with loved ones, or even as a crunchy dessert. Join me in exploring the flavors of Nigeria as we embark on the journey of making these cherished cookies.

**Prep Time: 20 mins**
**Cooking Time: 20 mins**
**Yields: 4 dozen cookies**

*Ingredients:*
2 cups all-purpose flour
1/4 cup granulated sugar
1/2 teaspoon ground nutmeg
1/4 teaspoon salt
1/4 cup unsalted butter, cold and diced
1/4 cup whole milk
1 large egg
1 teaspoon pure vanilla extract
Vegetable oil, for frying

*Directions:*
- In a large mixing bowl, combine the all-purpose flour, granulated sugar, ground nutmeg, and salt. Mix these dry ingredients thoroughly.
- Add the cold, diced unsalted butter to the dry ingredients. Using your fingertips, work the butter into the flour mixture until it resembles coarse breadcrumbs. This step is crucial for achieving the desired crispness in your Chin-Chin cookies.
- In a separate small bowl, whisk together the whole milk, large egg, and pure vanilla extract until well combined.
- Make a well in the center of the dry ingredients mixture, and pour the milk, egg, and vanilla mixture into it. Gradually incorporate the wet ingredients into the dry mixture, kneading gently until a smooth dough forms. Be careful not to over-knead, as it can make the cookies tough.

- On a clean, floured surface, roll out the dough to a thickness of about 1/4 inch. For this, a rolling pin can be used.
- Cut the rolled-out dough into small, bite-sized squares or rectangles using a knife or a cookie cutter. You can make them as small or as large as you prefer.
- In a deep saucepan or frying pan, heat vegetable oil over medium heat until it reaches 350°F (175°C). Carefully place a few pieces of the cut dough into the hot oil, ensuring not to overcrowd the pan.
- Fry the Chin-Chin cookies until they turn golden brown and crisp, usually about 3-4 minutes. Keep in mind to occasionally turn them for even cooking.
- Using a slotted spoon, remove the fried cookies from the hot oil and place them on paper towels to drain any excess oil.
- Allow the Chin-Chin cookies to cool completely before serving. They will continue to firm up as they cool, achieving that perfect crisp texture.

## Ma'amoul (North Africa)

Ma'amoul are shortbread-like cookies filled with dates, nuts, or figs. They are popular in North African countries like Egypt and Morocco.

**Prep Time:** 30 min
**Cooking Time:** 20 min
**Yields:** 20

*Ingredients:*
**For the Dough:**
2 cups semolina flour
1 cup clarified butter (ghee), melted and cooled
1/4 cup powdered sugar
1/4 cup rosewater or orange blossom water (for flavor)
1/4 teaspoon baking powder

**For the Filling:**
1 cup dates, pitted and chopped
1/2 cup mixed nuts (such as walnuts, pistachios, or almonds), finely chopped
2 tablespoons powdered sugar
1/2 teaspoon ground cinnamon
1/4 teaspoon ground cardamom
1/4 teaspoon orange zest (optional)

**For Dusting:**
Powdered sugar, for dusting (optional)

*Directions:*
**-Prepare the Filling:**
In a mixing bowl, combine the chopped dates, mixed nuts, powdered sugar, ground cinnamon, ground cardamom, and orange zest (if using). Mix well until the filling mixture is cohesive and holds together. Set aside.

**Prepare the Dough:**
- In a large mixing bowl, combine the semolina flour and baking powder.

- Slowly pour in the melted and cooled clarified butter (ghee) while continuously mixing the ingredients.
- Add the powdered sugar and rosewater or orange blossom water to the mixture, and knead everything together until a soft, pliable dough forms. If needed, add a little more rosewater or water to achieve the right consistency.

**Shape the Ma'amoul:**
- Take a small portion of the dough and shape it into a small ball, about the size of a walnut.
- Flatten the dough ball into the palm of your hand, creating a small, circular disc.
- Place a teaspoon of the prepared date and nut filling in the center of the disc.
- Carefully encase the filling with the dough, forming a ball or another desired shape. You can use special Ma'amoul molds for intricate designs if you have them.

**Bake the Ma'amoul:**
- Preheat your oven to 350°F (175°C).
- Arrange the shaped Ma'amoul cookies on a baking sheet lined with parchment paper.
- Bake in the preheated oven for 15-20 minutes, or until they turn a light golden brown.

**Cool and Serve:**
- Allow the baked Ma'amoul to cool on a wire rack for a few minutes.
- Optionally, dust the cooled Ma'amoul with powdered sugar for a touch of sweetness and decoration.
- Serve these delightful North African Ma'amoul cookies with a cup of aromatic tea or coffee and savor the blend of nutty fillings and crumbly, fragrant dough.

# Kahk (Egyptian Eid Cookie):

Kahk are traditional Egyptian cookies often made during celebrations like Eid-ul-Fitr. These buttery cookies are filled with dates and coated with powdered sugar.

**Prep Time: 30 mins**
**Cooking Time: 20 mins**
**Yields: 24 Kahk cookies**

*Ingredients:*
**For the Dough:**
3 cups all-purpose flour
1 cup unsalted butter, softened
1/2 cup powdered sugar
1 teaspoon vanilla extract
1 teaspoon baking powder
1/4 cup milk

**For the Filling:**
1 cup dates, pitted and finely chopped
1/2 cup mixed nuts (e.g., walnuts, almonds), finely chopped
1 teaspoon ground cinnamon
1/4 teaspoon ground cloves
1/4 teaspoon ground cardamom

**For Dusting:**
Powdered sugar

*Directions:*
**Prepare the Dough:**
In a large mixing bowl, combine the softened butter and powdered sugar. Cream them together until the mixture is light and fluffy. Add the vanilla extract and mix well. In a separate bowl, sift together the all-purpose flour and baking powder.
Gradually add the dry ingredients to the butter mixture, mixing until a crumbly texture forms.
Slowly incorporate the milk into the dough, kneading gently until it comes together to form a soft, smooth dough.

**Prepare the Filling:**
In a separate bowl, mix the finely chopped dates, mixed nuts, ground cinnamon, ground cloves, and ground cardamom. This will be the filling for your Kahk.

**Shape the Kahk:**
- Set a baking sheet on your oven's 350°F (180°C) setting and prepare your oven.
- Pinch off small portions of the dough and roll them into balls, roughly the size of a walnut.
- Flatten each dough ball in the palm of your hand and place a small amount of the date-nut filling in the center.
- Encase the filling with the dough, shaping it into a ball again. Ensure there are no cracks.
- Use a Kahk mold or the back of a fork to create decorative patterns on the surface of each cookie.

**Bake the Kahk:**
- Place the shaped Kahk cookies on the prepared baking sheet, leaving a bit of space between them.
- Bake in the preheated oven for approximately 20 minutes or until they turn a light golden color.

**Finish and Dust:**
- Remove the Kahk from the oven and allow them to cool on a wire rack.
- While they are still warm, dust the tops generously with powdered sugar. The sugar will adhere to the buttery surface, creating a delightful sweetness.

**Serve and Enjoy:**
- Once completely cooled, your Kahk cookies are ready to be savored. Enjoy the delightful flavors and cultural richness of this Egyptian treat with a cup of tea or coffee.

## Biskut Kenyah (Kenya):

Biskut Kenyah, or Kenyan cookies, are a delightful treat enjoyed by many in the beautiful landscapes of Kenya. These cookies are known for their simplicity and the way they capture the essence of Kenyan cuisine. With a subtle blend of spices and a satisfying crunch, Biskut Kenyah are perfect for dipping into a cup of Kenyan tea or enjoying as a snack any time of day.

**Prep Time: 20 mins**
**Cooking Time: 15 mins**
**Yields: 24 cookies**

*Ingredients:*
1 cup all-purpose flour
1/2 cup granulated sugar
1/4 teaspoon ground cardamom
1/4 teaspoon ground cinnamon
1/4 teaspoon ground cloves
1/4 teaspoon baking soda
Pinch of salt
1/2 cup unsalted butter, softened
1 egg yolk
1 teaspoon vanilla extract

*Directions:*
- **Preheat the Oven:** Preheat your oven to 350°F (180°C). Use parchment paper to line a baking sheet or gently oil it.
- **Sift the Dry Ingredients:** In a medium-sized bowl, sift together the all-purpose flour, granulated sugar, ground cardamom, ground cinnamon, ground cloves, baking soda, and a pinch of salt. Sifting helps ensure a uniform texture in the cookies.
- **Combine Butter and Sugar:** In a separate large bowl, cream the softened unsalted butter with the sugar until the mixture becomes light and fluffy. This should take about 2-3 minutes.
- **Add Egg Yolk and Vanilla:** Add the egg yolk and vanilla extract to the butter-sugar mixture. Mix well until fully incorporated.
- **Incorporate Dry Ingredients:** Gradually add the sifted dry ingredients into the wet mixture. Stir until a smooth dough forms. You may need to use your hands to fully combine the ingredients into a cohesive dough.
- **Shape the Cookies:** Take small portions of the dough and roll them into 1-inch balls. Place the balls on the prepared baking sheet, leaving a bit of space between each one. Use a fork to gently flatten each ball and create a crisscross pattern on top.
- **Bake:** Place the baking sheet in the preheated oven and bake for approximately 12-15 minutes or until the cookies turn golden brown around the edges.
- **Cool:** Once the cookies are done baking, remove them from the oven and allow them to cool on the baking sheet for a few minutes. Then, move them to a wire rack to cool entirely.
- **Enjoy:** Your Biskut Kenyah (Kenyan Cookies) are now ready to be enjoyed! Serve them with a cup of tea or as a delightful snack.

## Koeksisters (South Africa)

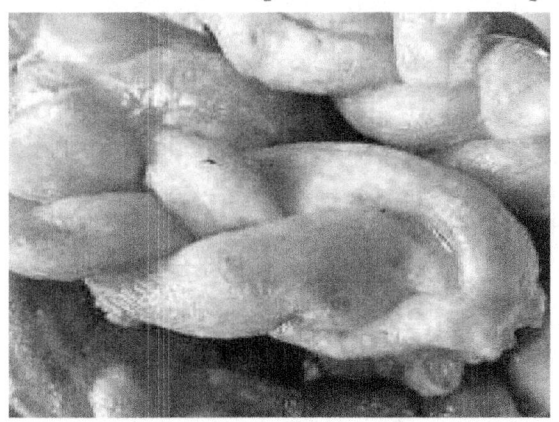

Koeksisters, a beloved South African treat, are a delectable combination of deep-fried dough, sweet syrup, and a hint of spice. These twisted and syrup-soaked pastries have a unique texture that's crisp on the outside and delightfully syrupy on the inside. Koeksisters have a special place in the hearts of South Africans, often enjoyed at celebrations, family gatherings, or as an indulgent afternoon snack. In this recipe, we'll guide you through the process of making these sweet delicacies, bringing a taste of South Africa to your kitchen.

**Prep Time: 20 mins**
**Cooking Time: 20 mins**
**Yields: 24 Koeksisters**

*Ingredients:*
**For the Dough:**
2 cups all-purpose flour
2 teaspoons baking powder
A pinch of salt
2 tablespoons cold butter, cubed
2/3 cup milk

**For the Syrup:**
2 cups white sugar
1 1/2 cups water
1 cinnamon stick
2-3 strips of lemon zest
A pinch of ground ginger

**For Frying:**
Vegetable oil for deep frying

*Directions:*
**Prepare the Dough:**
- In a large mixing bowl, combine the flour, baking powder, and a pinch of salt.
- Add the cold, cubed butter to the dry ingredients.
- Use your fingers to rub the butter into the flour until the mixture resembles coarse breadcrumbs.
- Gradually add the milk while mixing until you have a soft, pliable dough.
- Knead the dough on a floured surface for a few minutes until smooth.
- Cover the dough with a clean kitchen towel and let it rest for 15 minutes.

**Shape the Koeksisters:**
- Roll out the dough to about 1/4 inch (6mm) thickness.
- Cut the dough into strips, approximately 3 inches long and 1/2 inch wide.
- Make a lengthwise slit in the center of each strip, leaving the top and bottom edges intact.
- Carefully twist each strip, creating a twisted, braided shape, and pinch the ends together.

**Prepare the Syrup:**
- In a saucepan, combine the sugar, water, cinnamon stick, lemon zest strips, and a pinch of ground ginger.
- Bring the mixture to a boil while stirring to ensure that the sugar dissolves fully.
- Reduce the heat and let the syrup simmer for about 10 minutes, allowing it to thicken slightly.
- Remove the cinnamon stick and lemon zest, and set the syrup aside to cool.

**Fry the Koeksisters:**
- Heat vegetable oil in a deep frying pan or pot to 350°F (180°C).
- Carefully place a few twisted dough pieces into the hot oil and fry until they are deep golden brown and crisp, about 2-3 minutes per side.
- Using a slotted spoon, remove the fried Koeksisters from the oil and drain them on paper towels.

- While still hot, immerse the Koeksisters in the cooled syrup, ensuring they are well coated.
- Allow them to soak for a few minutes, turning them occasionally to absorb the syrup.

**Serve and Enjoy:**
- Once fully soaked and syrupy, remove the Koeksisters from the syrup and place them on a wire rack to cool and allow any excess syrup to drip off.
- Koeksisters are best enjoyed when still slightly warm, so dig in and savor the sweet, sticky, and spiced goodness of South Africa.

## Namibian Ginger Biscuits

Namibia, a land of stunning desert landscapes and rich cultural diversity, offers a unique twist on the classic ginger biscuit. These Namibian Ginger Biscuits are a delightful fusion of bold ginger flavors and the warmth of traditional Namibian hospitality. Perfect for sharing with friends or enjoying with a cup of tea, these biscuits will transport your taste buds to the heart of Africa.

**Prep: 15 mins**
**Cooking Time: 15 mins**
**Yields: 24 biscuits**

*Ingredients:*
1 1/2 cups all-purpose flour
1 teaspoon baking soda
1 teaspoon ground ginger
1/2 teaspoon ground cinnamon
1/4 teaspoon ground cloves
1/4 teaspoon salt
1/2 cup unsalted butter, softened
1/2 cup granulated sugar
1/2 cup brown sugar, packed
1/4 cup molasses
1 large egg
1 teaspoon pure vanilla extract
1/4 cup crystallized ginger, finely chopped (optional, for extra zing)
Additional granulated sugar, for rolling

*Directions:*
- **Preheat the Oven:** Preheat your oven to 350°F (180°C). Set aside two baking sheets that have been lined with parchment paper.
- **Sift Dry Ingredients:** In a medium-sized mixing bowl, sift together the all-purpose flour, baking soda, ground ginger, ground cinnamon, ground cloves, and salt. Set this dry mixture aside.
- **Cream the Butter and Sugars:** In a separate large mixing bowl, cream together the softened butter, granulated sugar, and brown sugar until the mixture is light and fluffy. This can take about 2-3 minutes.
- **Incorporate Wet Ingredients:** To the creamed butter and sugar mixture, add the molasses, large egg, and pure vanilla extract. Mix until well combined.
- **Combine Dry and Wet Mixtures:** Gradually add the dry ingredient mixture to the wet ingredients. Mix until a smooth dough forms. If desired, fold in the finely

chopped crystallized ginger for an extra burst of ginger flavor.
- **Shape Dough into Balls:** Roll tablespoons of the dough into small balls using your hands. Then, roll each ball in additional granulated sugar to coat them evenly.
- **Arrange on Baking Sheets:** Place the sugar-coated dough balls onto the prepared baking sheets, leaving enough space between each for them to spread during baking.
- **Bake:** Bake the biscuits in the preheated oven for approximately 12-15 minutes or until the edges turn golden brown.
- **Cool and Enjoy:** Remove the biscuits from the oven and allow them to cool on the baking sheets for a few minutes before transferring them to a wire rack to cool completely. Once cooled, savor the unique flavors of Namibia with these delectable ginger biscuits.

## Mandazi (East Africa)

Mandazi is a delightful fried dough pastry that has captured the hearts and taste buds of many. Known for its golden, slightly crispy exterior and soft, pillowy interior, Mandazi is a popular treat enjoyed across the region. In this recipe, we'll guide you through the process of creating these delectable delights in the comfort of your own kitchen.

**Prep Time:** 15 mins
**Cooking Time:** 15 mins
**Yields:** Approximately 12 Mandazi

*Ingredients:*
2 cups all-purpose flour
1/4 cup granulated sugar
1/2 teaspoon ground cardamom (for a subtle hint of spice)
1/4 teaspoon salt
1 teaspoon baking powder
1/2 cup coconut milk (or regular milk)
1 egg
2 tablespoons melted butter or vegetable oil
Oil for frying

*Directions:*
- **Prepare the Dough:** In a large mixing bowl, combine the all-purpose flour, granulated sugar, ground cardamom, salt, and baking powder. These dry components should be thoroughly combined.
- **Create the Wet Mixture:** In a separate bowl, whisk together the coconut milk (or regular milk), egg, and melted butter or vegetable oil until the mixture is smooth and well combined.
- **Combine the Mixtures:** Gradually pour the wet mixture into the dry ingredients. Stir the mixture with a wooden spoon or spatula until it forms a soft, sticky dough. If the dough is too dry, add a little more milk; if it's too wet, add a touch more flour.
- **Knead the Dough:** Turn the dough out onto a lightly floured surface and knead it gently for about 5 minutes until it becomes smooth and elastic. This step helps develop the Mandazi's texture.

- **Shape the Mandazi:** Roll the dough out to a thickness of about 1/4 inch and cut it into desired shapes—traditionally, Mandazi are cut into triangles or squares.
- **Heat the Oil:** In a deep frying pan or pot, heat enough oil for frying over medium-high heat. You'll know it's ready when a small piece of dough sizzles and rises to the surface when added to the oil.
- **Fry the Mandazi:** Carefully place the Mandazi pieces into the hot oil, being cautious not to overcrowd the pan. Fry them until they turn golden brown on both sides, usually about 2-3 minutes per side. With the help of a slotted spoon, take them from the oil and set them on a plate covered with paper towels so that any extra oil may drip out.
- **Serve Warm:** Mandazi are best enjoyed fresh and warm. They can be served plain or dusted with powdered sugar for an extra touch of sweetness.

## Kulikuli (West Africa)

Kulikuli are crunchy, peanut-based snacks that are commonly enjoyed in West African countries such as Nigeria and Ghana. Kulikuli, the beloved snack of West Africa, is a delectable treat that combines the rich flavors of groundnuts (peanuts) with a delightful crunch. It's a popular street food, a flavorful appetizer, and a cherished companion for any gathering. In this recipe, we'll explore how to make this beloved West African delicacy from scratch.

**Prep Time: 15 mins**
**Cooking Time: 25 mins**
**Yields: 20 pieces**

*Ingredients:*
2 cups raw groundnuts (peanuts)
2 cloves garlic, minced
1 teaspoon cayenne pepper (adjust to taste)
1 teaspoon salt
1/2 teaspoon paprika
1/4 cup water
Vegetable oil for frying

*Directions:*
**Prepare the Groundnuts:**
- Begin by roasting the raw groundnuts. Place them in a dry, hot skillet or frying pan over medium heat.
- Stir the groundnuts frequently to ensure even roasting. They are ready when they turn golden brown and emit a rich, nutty aroma.
- Remove the roasted groundnuts from the heat and let them cool. Once cooled, rub the groundnuts between your palms to remove the outer skins. You can also use a clean kitchen towel to help with this process.

**Prepare the Paste:**
- In a food processor, combine the peeled groundnuts, minced garlic, cayenne pepper, salt, and paprika.
- Pulse the ingredients until a thick paste forms. You may need to scrape down the sides of the processor bowl occasionally to ensure even blending.

**Add Water:**

- With the food processor running, gradually add the water. This will help bind the ingredients together and create a smoother, dough-like consistency.

**Shape the Kulikuli:**
- Take small portions of the peanut mixture and shape them into bite-sized balls or oval shapes. You can also use cookie cutters for more intricate designs if desired.

**Heat the Oil:**
- Warm up the vegetable oil in a large saucepan or frying pan over medium heat. To test if the oil is hot enough, drop a small piece of the peanut mixture into the oil. If it sizzles and rises to the surface, the oil is ready for frying.

**Fry the Kulikuli:**
- Carefully place the shaped kulikuli pieces into the hot oil, making sure not to overcrowd the pan.
- Fry the kulikuli until they turn a deep golden brown, which should take about 3-5 minutes. Ensure they cook evenly by flipping them occasionally with a slotted spoon.

**Drain and Cool:**
- Once the kulikuli have reached the desired golden color, use a slotted spoon to remove them from the hot oil. To drain the extra oil, put them on a dish covered with paper towels.

**Enjoy Your Kulikuli:**
- Allow the kulikuli to cool completely before indulging in this West African delight. Share them with friends and family, or savor them as a snack all to yourself.

# Baklava (North Africa)

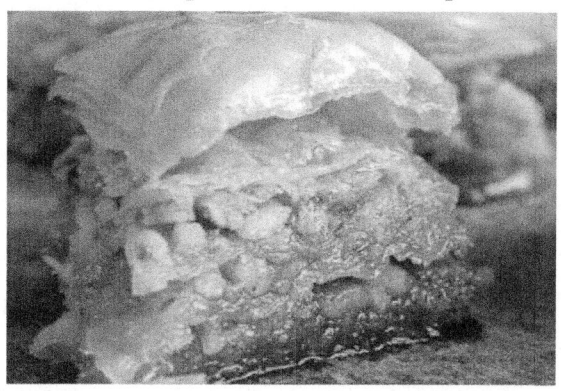

Baklava is a sweet pastry made of layers of filo dough, filled with chopped nuts, and sweetened with syrup or honey. It is popular in North African countries with Mediterranean influences.

**Prep Time: 30 mins**
**Cooking Time: 45 mins**
**Yields: 24 pieces**

*Ingredients:*
**For the Baklava:**
2 cups of coarsely chopped mixed nuts (including walnuts, pistachios, and almonds) and 1 package (16 ounces) of frozen phyllo dough
1 cup (2 sticks) of unsalted butter, melted
1 teaspoon ground cinnamon
1/2 teaspoon ground cloves

**For the Syrup:**
1 cup granulated sugar
1/2 cup water
1/2 cup honey
1 teaspoon vanilla extract
1 lemon, zest and juice
1 cinnamon stick

*Directions:*
**Prepare the Syrup:**

- In a saucepan, combine sugar, water, honey, vanilla extract, lemon zest, lemon juice, and the cinnamon stick.
- Over medium-high heat, bring the mixture to a boil while stirring until the sugar dissolves.
- Reduce heat and simmer for 10-15 minutes, or until the syrup thickens slightly.
- Remove from heat and let it cool. Discard the cinnamon stick.

**Preheat the Oven:**
- Preheat your oven to 350°F (175°C). Grease a 9x13-inch (23x33 cm) baking dish with melted butter.

**Prepare the Nut Mixture:**
- In a mixing bowl, combine the finely chopped nuts, ground cinnamon, and ground cloves. Set aside.

**Assemble the Layers:**
- Lay one sheet of phyllo dough in the prepared baking dish and brush it with melted butter.
- Repeat this process, layering and buttering each sheet until you have about 8 sheets layered.

**Add the Nut Filling:**
- Sprinkle a generous portion of the nut mixture evenly over the phyllo layers.

**Continue Layering:**
- Layer another 4-5 sheets of phyllo, buttering each sheet as before.

**Add More Nuts:**
- Sprinkle another layer of the nut mixture on top of the phyllo layers.

**Finish with Phyllo:**
- Layer the remaining phyllo sheets, continuing to butter each one.

**Cut into Diamonds:**
- Carefully cut the Baklava into diamond or square shapes using a sharp knife.

**Bake:**
- Place the baking dish in the preheated oven and bake for approximately 45 minutes or until the Baklava is golden brown and crisp.

**Pour the Syrup:**
- As soon as the Baklava is out of the oven, immediately pour the cooled syrup evenly over the hot pastry. Allow it to absorb the syrup for a few hours or overnight.

**Serve:**
- Once the Baklava has fully absorbed the syrup and cooled, it's ready to be enjoyed. Serve it as a sweet treat with a hint of North African flair.

## Kletskoppen (South Africa)

Kletskoppen, a beloved South African treat, embodies the essence of simple yet delightful baking. Kletskoppen are thin, crispy almond cookies that are a sweet delight in South Africa. They are often enjoyed with coffee.

**Prep Time: 15 minS**
**Cooking Time: 15 minutes**
**Yields: 24 Kletskoppen**

*Ingredients:*
1 cup granulated sugar
1 cup all-purpose flour
1/2 cup unsalted butter, melted
1/4 cup milk
1/2 teaspoon vanilla extract
A pinch of salt

*Directions:*
- **Preheat and Prepare:** Preheat your oven to 350°F (175°C) and line a baking sheet with parchment paper. Ensure your oven rack is in the middle position.
- **Combine Sugar and Flour:** In a mixing bowl, combine the granulated sugar and all-purpose flour. Stir them together until well-mixed.
- **Add Melted Butter:** Pour the melted unsalted butter into the dry mixture. Stir until the butter is fully incorporated, and the mixture resembles coarse crumbs.
- **Add Milk and Vanilla:** Gradually pour in the milk and add the vanilla extract to the mixture. Stir until a smooth batter forms. The batter will be thin.
- **Shape the Kletskoppen:** Using a teaspoon, drop small amounts of the batter onto the prepared baking sheet, leaving plenty of space between them. These cookies will spread while baking, so make sure to leave enough room.
- **Bake to Perfection:** Place the baking sheet in the preheated oven and bake for approximately 12-15 minutes or until the Kletskoppen are golden brown. Keep a close eye on them during the last few minutes, as they can quickly go from golden to over-baked.
- **Cool and Enjoy:** Once baked to perfection, remove the Kletskoppen from the oven and let them cool on the baking sheet for a couple of minutes. They will firm up as they cool. After that, move them to a wire rack to finish cooling.
- **Serve:** Kletskoppen are best enjoyed with a cup of tea or coffee. Their delicate crispiness and caramelized sweetness make them an ideal companion for your afternoon break.

# CHAPTER 6: OCEANIC COOKIE BLISS

## Australian Anzac Biscuits

The Anzac biscuit is a cherished Australian icon, with a history that dates back to World War I. Named after the Australian and New Zealand Army Corps (ANZAC), these hearty oat-based biscuits were sent to soldiers on the front lines. Today, they remain a symbol of resilience and the enduring Australian spirit. In this recipe, we'll recreate this classic treat and pay tribute to the brave men and women who served their country.

**Prep Time:** 15 mins
**Cooking Time:** 15 mins
**Yields:** 20 biscuits

*Ingredients:*
1 cup rolled oats
1 cup plain flour
1 cup desiccated coconut
3/4 cup granulated sugar
1/2 cup unsalted butter
2 tablespoons golden syrup (or substitute with honey)
1/2 teaspoon baking soda
2 tablespoons boiling water

*Directions:*
- **Preheat and Prepare:** Preheat your oven to 325°F (160°C) and line a baking tray with parchment paper.
- **Combine Dry Ingredients:** In a large mixing bowl, combine the rolled oats, plain flour, desiccated coconut, and granulated sugar. Mix well.
- **Melt Butter and Syrup:** In a saucepan over low heat, melt the unsalted butter and golden syrup (or honey) together. Stir until well combined.
- **Dissolve Baking Soda:** In a small bowl, mix the baking soda with the boiling water until it dissolves.
- **Combine Wet Ingredients:** Pour the melted butter and syrup mixture into the dry ingredients. Add the dissolved baking soda and water mixture. Stir until all the ingredients are well combined, creating a sticky dough.
- **Form Biscuits:** Take spoonfuls of the mixture and roll them into small balls. Leave adequate room between each one when you put them on the baking sheet that has been prepared.
- **Flatten Biscuits:** Gently press each dough ball with the back of a fork. The texture of the biscuits will be determined by this.
- **Bake:** Put the biscuits on a baking sheet in the preheated oven, and bake for 12 to 15 minutes, or until golden brown. Watch them carefully to avoid overbaking.
- **Cool and Enjoy:** Remove the Anzac biscuits from the oven and allow them to cool on the baking tray for a few minutes before transferring them to a wire rack to cool completely. Once cooled, enjoy your homemade Anzac biscuits with a cup of tea or coffee.

## New Zealand Kiwi Shortbread

New Zealand Kiwi Shortbread is a delightful twist on the classic shortbread cookie, infusing the rich buttery goodness with the vibrant flavors of New Zealand's beloved fruit, the kiwi. These cookies are a true kiwi experience, offering a sweet and tangy taste of the Kiwi countryside in every bite.

**Prep Time:** 20 mins
**Cooking Time:** 15 mins

**Yields: 24 cookies**

*Ingredients:*

1 cup (2 sticks) unsalted butter, softened
1/2 cup confectioners' sugar (powdered sugar)
2 cups all-purpose flour
1/2 cup cornstarch
1/2 teaspoon salt
2 ripe kiwis, peeled and finely diced
Zest of 1 kiwi (optional, for extra flavor)
Additional powdered sugar for dusting (optional)

*Directions:*

- **Preheat the Oven:** Set the Oven to 325°F (160°C) and line a baking sheet with parchment paper.
- **Cream the Butter and Sugar:** Place the softened butter and confectioners' sugar in a mixing dish and beat until frothy. Use a wooden spoon or an electric mixer for this phase, which usually takes two to three minutes.
- **Sift dry ingredients:** Combine all-purpose flour, cornstarch, and salt in a separate bowl. Your shortbread will have a more fragile and delicate texture thanks to sifting.
- **Combine Wet and Dry Ingredients:** Add the dry ingredients, which have been sifted, gradually to the butter-sugar mixture. Mix until a cohesive ball of dough forms from the ingredients.
  Be careful not to overmix; stop as soon as the ingredients are combined.
- **Add Kiwi:** Gently fold in the diced kiwis and, if desired, the kiwi zest. The kiwis will add a delightful burst of flavor and a touch of tartness to the cookies.
- **Shape the Cookies:** On a lightly floured surface, roll the dough into a log shape, about 2 inches in diameter. You can also use cookie cutters if you prefer different shapes. For a traditional shortbread look, you can simply slice the log into rounds.
- **Bake:** Place the shaped cookies onto the prepared baking sheet, leaving a bit of space between each one. Bake in the preheated oven for approximately 15 minutes or until the edges turn lightly golden. Keep a close eye on them to prevent over-baking, as shortbread should remain pale in color.
- **Cool and Dust:** Allow the cookies to cool on a wire rack for a few minutes. If desired, dust them with a little extra powdered sugar for a sweet finishing touch.
- **Serve and Enjoy:** Your New Zealand Kiwi Shortbread is now ready to be savored. Enjoy these delightful cookies with a cup of tea or as a sweet treat any time of day.

## Hawaiian Coconut Macadamia Cookies

Transport your taste buds to the tropical paradise of Hawaii with our Hawaiian Coconut Macadamia Cookies. These delightful cookies capture the essence of the Hawaiian islands with their rich, buttery flavor, crunchy macadamia nuts, and sweet coconut. Whether you've been to Hawaii or dream of going, these cookies will make you feel like you're lounging on a sun-kissed beach with each bite.

**Prep Time: 15 mins**
**Cooking Time: 15 mins**
**Yields: 24 cookies**

*Ingredients:*
1 cup (2 sticks) unsalted butter, softened
1 cup granulated sugar
1 cup packed light brown sugar
2 large eggs
1 teaspoon pure vanilla extract
2 1/2 cups all-purpose flour
1 teaspoon baking soda
1/2 teaspoon salt
1 cup sweetened shredded coconut
1 cup chopped macadamia nuts
1/2 cup white chocolate chips (optional, for extra indulgence)

*Directions:*
- **Preheat the Oven:** Preheat your oven to 350°F (180°C). Two baking pans should be lightly greased or lined with parchment paper.
- **Cream the Butter and Sugars:** In a large mixing bowl, combine the softened butter, light brown sugar, and granulated sugar and beat until well-combined and fluffy. Usually, using an electric mixer set to medium speed, this takes two to three minutes.
- **Add Eggs and Vanilla:** Beat in the eggs and vanilla one at a time, making sure each egg is well mixed before adding the next. Mix well after adding the vanilla extract.
- **Combine Dry Ingredients:** In a separate dish, mash the salt, baking soda, and all-purpose flour together.
- **Gradually Add Dry Ingredients:** Gradually add the dry ingredients to the butter-sugar mixture, mixing on low speed until just combined. Be careful not to overmix; you want the dough to come together without being overworked.
- **Fold in Coconut and Macadamia Nuts:** Gently fold in the shredded coconut, chopped macadamia nuts, and white chocolate chips (if using). This will give your cookies that signature Hawaiian flair.
- **Shape and Bake:** Drop rounded tablespoons of cookie dough onto the prepared baking sheets, spacing them about 2 inches apart. You can use a cookie scoop for even portions. With the back of a spoon or your fingertips, slightly flatten each cookie.
- **Bake:** Place the baking trays in the preheated oven and bake for 12 to 15 minutes, or until the centers are firm and the borders are golden brown. Do not overbake the cookies since they will continue to firm up as they cool.
- **Cool and Enjoy:** After a few minutes on the baking pans, remove the cookies to wire racks to finish cooling. Once cooled, savor the taste of Hawaii in every bite!

# Fijian Taro Root Cookies

Taro, a starchy and slightly nutty root vegetable, takes center stage in this unique cookie recipe. These cookies offer a delightful combination of earthy taro, sweet coconut, and a hint of tropical fruitiness, making them a true Fijian delight.

**Prep Time: 20 mins**
**Cooking Time: 15 mins**
**Yields: 24 cookies**

### Ingredients:

1 cup taro root, boiled and mashed
1/2 cup unsalted butter, softened
1/2 cup granulated sugar
1/4 cup coconut milk
1/4 cup shredded coconut
1 teaspoon vanilla extract
2 cups all-purpose flour
1/2 teaspoon baking powder
A pinch of salt

### Directions:

- Begin by peeling, chopping, and boiling the taro root until it becomes tender. Drain and mash it into a smooth consistency. Set aside to cool.
- In a mixing bowl, cream together the softened butter and granulated sugar until light and fluffy. This may take about 2-3 minutes of mixing.
- Gradually add the mashed taro root to the butter-sugar mixture, ensuring it's well incorporated. The vibrant purple color of the taro will infuse the dough, giving it a unique hue.
- Stir in the coconut milk, shredded coconut, and vanilla extract, blending until all the ingredients are thoroughly combined.
- In a separate bowl, whisk together the all-purpose flour, baking powder, and a pinch of salt. Gradually add this dry mixture to the wet ingredients, mixing until a dough forms. Avoid over-mixing, and stop as soon as the dough comes together.
The dough should be formed into a log, covered with plastic wrap, and chilled for at least 30 minutes. The dough will be simpler to handle after being chilled.
- Set a baking sheet on your oven's 350°F (175°C) rack and preheat the oven.
- Depending on your desire, slice the cold dough into rounds or roll it into little balls. Place these, spacing the cookies apart, on the baking sheet that has been prepared.
- Bake the cookies in the preheated oven for 12 to 15 minutes, or until the edges are golden brown.
- The cookies should be taken out of the oven and allowed to cool on a wire rack. As they cool, they will firm up and develop their unique taro flavor.
- Once completely cooled, these Fijian Taro Root Cookies are ready to delight your taste buds with their exotic combination of flavors. Enjoy them as a tropical snack or a sweet treat with a cup of tea, and savor the taste of Fiji in every bite.

# CHAPTER 7: ANTARCTICA-INSPIRED ICEBOX COOKIES

## Iced Blueberry Glacier Cookies

These cookies are a delightful blend of sweet and tangy flavors, reminiscent of the blueberry-studded glaciers that dot the landscape. Whether you're indulging in a midday snack or sharing them with loved ones, these cookies will transport you to a world of frosty wonder.

**Prep Time: 15 mins**
**Cooking Time: 12-15 mins**
**Yields: 24 cookies**

*Ingredients:*
1 cup unsalted butter, softened
1 cup granulated sugar
2 large eggs
2 teaspoons pure vanilla extract
2 1/2 cups all-purpose flour
1 teaspoon baking powder
1/2 teaspoon salt
1/2 cup freeze-dried blueberries, crushed
1/2 cup confectioners' sugar
2 tablespoons lemon juice
Zest of one lemon
Blue food coloring (optional)

*Directions:*
- Set a baking sheet on your oven's 350°F (175°C) rack and preheat the oven.
The softened butter and granulated sugar should be creamed for two to three minutes in a large mixing basin.
- One at a time, add the eggs, beating well after each addition. Add the vanilla essence and stir.
- The all-purpose flour, baking soda, and salt should be combined in a separate basin.
- As you gradually combine the dry and liquid components, a nice cookie dough will develop.
- Gently fold in the crushed freeze-dried blueberries, giving the dough a beautiful natural hue and a burst of fruity flavor.
- Scoop out tablespoon-sized portions of cookie dough and roll them into balls. Place them on the prepared baking sheet, spacing them about 2 inches apart.
- Using the bottom of a glass or a cookie press, gently flatten each cookie ball to your desired thickness, creating a smooth, round surface.
- Bake in the preheated oven for 12-15 minutes or until the edges turn lightly golden.
- While the cookies are cooling on a wire rack, prepare the icing. Confectioners sugar, lemon juice, and lemon zest are combined in a small bowl. If desired, add a drop or two of blue food coloring for a glacier-like appearance.
- Once the cookies have cooled completely, drizzle or spread the icing over the tops of the cookies, allowing it to set for a few minutes.

- Serve your Iced Blueberry Glacier Cookies with a warm beverage or enjoy them as a delightful standalone treat. These cookies are sure to transport your taste buds to the frosty beauty of Antarctica with every bite.

## Polar Bear Pawprint Cookies

Polar Bear Pawprint Cookies are a whimsical addition to your cookie repertoire, inspired by the frosty beauty of Antarctica. These adorable treats capture the essence of the icy landscape with their snowy white exterior and playful pawprint design. Perfect for winter gatherings, holiday parties, or simply when you want to bring a touch of Arctic charm to your dessert table, these cookies are as fun to make as they are to eat.

**Prep Time: 30 mins**
**Cooking Time: 10 mins**
**Yields: 24 cookies**

*Ingredients:*
1 cup unsalted butter, softened
1 cup confectioners' sugar
1 large egg
2 teaspoons pure vanilla extract
2 1/2 cups all-purpose flour
1/2 teaspoon salt
1/2 cup shredded coconut, sweetened
48 mini chocolate chips

*Directions:*
- **Preparation:** Preheat your oven to 350 degrees Fahrenheit (175 degrees Celsius), and line a baking sheet with parchment paper.
- **Cream Butter and Sugar:** In a large mixing bowl, cream together the softened butter and confectioners' sugar until light and fluffy. This should take about 2-3 minutes.
- **Add Egg and Vanilla:** Beat in the egg and vanilla extract until well incorporated.
- **Combine Dry Ingredients:** In a separate bowl, whisk together the flour and salt. Gradually add this dry mixture to the wet ingredients, mixing until a soft cookie dough forms.
- **Shape the Cookies:** Roll the cookie dough into 1-inch balls and place them on the prepared baking sheet, leaving a little space between each. With the palm of your hand, gently press each ball into the ground.
- **Create Pawprints:** To create the polar bear pawprints, gently press two mini chocolate chips into each cookie. Place them close together with the pointed ends touching, creating an oval shape.
- **Add Coconut Fur:** Carefully sprinkle shredded coconut around the chocolate chip pawprints to resemble the bear's furry coat.
- **Bake:** Bake the cookies in the preheated oven for approximately 10 minutes or until the edges are lightly golden.
- **Cool:** Let the cookies cool for a few minutes on the baking sheet before moving them to a wire rack to finish cooling.

- **Serve and Enjoy:** Once cooled, serve these adorable Polar Bear Pawprint Cookies to the delight of your family and friends. Watch their faces light up as they savor the playful charm and delicious flavor of these Arctic-inspired treats.

## Snowflake Cookies

Craft intricate snowflake-shaped cookies and decorate them with white or blue royal icing for a touch of Antarctic elegance. Snowflake cookies are a delightful winter treat that captures the magic of the season with their delicate appearance and sweet, buttery flavor. Whether you're looking to add a touch of whimsy to your holiday gatherings or simply craving a cozy baking project on a snowy day, these cookies are the perfect choice.

**Prep Time: 20 mins**
**Cooking Time: 12 mins per batch**
**Yields: 24 snowflake cookies**

*Ingredients:*
2 1/2 cups all-purpose flour
1/2 teaspoon baking powder
1/4 teaspoon salt
1 cup unsalted butter, softened
1 cup granulated sugar
1 large egg
1 teaspoon pure vanilla extract
(1/4 teaspoon optional, for taste) almond extract
Dusting with confectioners' sugar is optional.

*Directions:*
- Combine the all-purpose flour, baking soda, and salt in a medium basin. Place aside.
- Cream the softened unsalted butter and granulated sugar until frothy in a separate, large mixing dish. Using an electric mixer set on medium speed should take two to three minutes.
- To the butter-sugar mixture, add the egg, vanilla extract, and almond extract (if using). Beat consistently until everything is blended.
- Mixture of the dry components (from step 1) should be added to the wet ingredients gradually. Mix until dough starts to form. Don't over-mix; stop after all the ingredients are mixed.
- Each half of the dough should be formed into a disk. Refrigerate them for at least 30 minutes after wrapping them in plastic wrap. The dough will be simpler to handle after being chilled.
- Set a baking sheet on your oven's 350°F (175°C) rack and preheat the oven.
- On a lightly dusted surface, roll out one of the dough disks to a thickness of approximately 1/4 inch. Cut out your cookies using cookie cutters in the form of snowflakes. Leave some room between each snowflake as you arrange them on the baking sheet that has been prepared.

- Bake the cookies in the preheated oven for 10 to 12 minutes, or until the edges are lightly golden brown. Keep a close check on them because the size and thickness of your snowflakes may affect the baking time.
- Take the cookies out of the oven and allow them to cool for a few minutes on the baking sheet before transferring them to a wire rack to finish cooling.
- Once the cookies are completely cooled, you can dust them with confectioners' sugar for a snowy finish, if desired.

## CONVERSION CHART

### Volume Measurements:
1 teaspoon (tsp) = 5 milliliters (ml)
1 tablespoon (tbsp) = 15 milliliters (ml)
1 fluid ounce (fl oz) = 30 milliliters (ml)
1 cup (c) = 240 milliliters (ml)
1 pint (pt) = 480 milliliters (ml)
1 quart (qt) = 960 milliliters (ml)
1 gallon (gal) = 3.8 liters (L)

### Weight Measurements:
1 ounce (oz) = 28.35 grams (g)
1 pound (lb) = 16 ounces (oz) = 453.59 grams (g)
1 kilogram (kg) = 1,000 grams (g) = 2.205 pounds (lb)

### Temperature Conversions:
Celsius (°C) to Fahrenheit (°F): (°C × 9/5) + 32 = °F
Fahrenheit (°F) to Celsius (°C): (°F - 32) × 5/9 = °C

### Common Ingredient Conversions:
1 stick of butter = 1/2 cup = 8 tablespoons = 4 ounces = 113 grams
1 cup of all-purpose flour = 120 grams
1 cup of granulated sugar = 200 grams
1 cup of brown sugar (packed) = 220 grams
1 cup of powdered sugar = 125 grams
1 cup of oats = 90 grams
1 cup of chopped nuts = 120 grams
1 cup of chocolate chips = 175 grams
1 cup of raisins = 150 grams
1 cup of shredded coconut = 85 grams
1 cup of honey = 340 grams
1 cup of maple syrup = 322 grams
1 cup of milk = 240 milliliters (ml)
1 cup of heavy cream = 240 milliliters (ml)
1 cup of vegetable oil = 240 milliliters (ml)
1 cup of yogurt = 240 milliliters (ml)
1 tablespoon of baking powder = 15 grams
1 tablespoon of baking soda = 15 grams
1 tablespoon of salt = 18 grams
1 teaspoon of vanilla extract = 5 milliliters (ml)

### Baking Substitutions
**Butter:** Replace with an equal amount of margarine or vegetable shortening.
For a dairy-free option, use coconut oil, soy-based butter, or vegan butter.

**Eggs:** Substitute each egg with 1/4 cup unsweetened applesauce for moisture and binding.
Use a mashed ripe banana or 1/4 cup yogurt for binding in recipes.

For a vegan option, try commercial egg replacers like flax eggs, chia eggs, or aquafaba.

**Milk:** Swap regular milk with dairy-free alternatives like almond milk, soy milk, oat milk, or coconut milk.
Buttermilk can be mimicked by adding 1 tablespoon of vinegar or lemon juice to 1 cup of milk and letting it sit for a few minutes.

**All-Purpose Flour:** Use whole wheat flour for added fiber and nutrients.
For gluten-free baking, try almond flour, coconut flour, rice flour, or a gluten-free flour blend.

**Sugar:** Replace granulated sugar with brown sugar or vice versa, adjusting for flavor. Substitute white sugar with honey, maple syrup, agave nectar, or stevia for a healthier option. Coconut sugar is a less processed alternative to traditional sugars.

**Baking Powder:** Create homemade baking powder by mixing 1 part baking soda with 2 parts cream of tartar. Replace with self-rising flour and omit the baking powder and salt from the recipe.

**Baking Soda:** If you're out of baking soda, use 3 times the amount of baking powder as a replacement.

**Vanilla Extract:** Use almond extract, maple extract, or other flavored extracts for unique variations.
Vanilla bean paste or vanilla powder can also be used as substitutes.

**Chocolate Chips:** Swap chocolate chips with white chocolate chips, butterscotch chips, or dried fruits like raisins or cranberries.
Chopped nuts, such as walnuts or pecans, can provide a delightful crunch.

**Cocoa Powder:** Unsweetened cocoa powder can be replaced with unsweetened carob powder for a caffeine-free option.
Dark chocolate or semisweet chocolate chips can be melted and used as a substitute.

**Yoghourt:** Greek yoghurt can be replaced with regular yoghurt or sour cream.
For dairy-free options, try coconut yoghourt or almond yoghurt.

**Cream of Tartar:** Substitute cream of tartar with white vinegar or lemon juice when stabilising egg whites or making meringue.

**Cornstarch:** Arrowroot powder or potato starch can be used as a thickening agent in place of cornstarch.

## LIST OF INGREDIENTS

This list includes both common ingredients and specific ingredients mentioned in the book:

**All-purpose flour**
**Baking powder**
**Salt**
**Unsalted butter**
**Granulated sugar**
**Large egg**
**Pure vanilla extract**

| | |
|---|---|
| Almond extract (optional) | Buttermilk |
| Confectioners' sugar (optional) | Vinegar |
| Maple pecans | Lemon juice |
| Mexican wedding cookies | Whole wheat flour |
| Cranberry white chocolate cookies | Almond flour |
| Alfajores | Coconut flour |
| Brazilian brigadeiros | Rice flour |
| Peruvian polvorones | Gluten-free flour blend |
| Colombian arequipe thumbprint cookies | Honey |
| French macarons | Maple syrup |
| Italian amaretti cookies | Agave nectar |
| German Lebkuchen cookies | Stevia |
| Spanish almond tuiles | Coconut sugar |
| Russian tea cakes | Brown sugar |
| Chinese almond cookies | Cream of tartar |
| Japanese matcha shortbread | Baking soda |
| Indian nan khatai | Almond extract |
| Thai mango sticky rice cookies | Maple extract |
| Moroccan almond crescents | Coconut sugar |
| South African Hertzog cookies | Self-rising flour |
| Egyptian Basbousa cookies | Almond extract |
| Nigerian Chin-Chin cookies | Maple extract |
| Australian Anzac biscuits | Vanilla bean paste |
| New Zealand Kiwi shortbread | Vanilla powder |
| Hawaiian coconut macadamia cookies | White chocolate chips |
| Fijian taro root cookies | Butterscotch chips |
| Iced blueberry glacier cookies | Raisins |
| Polar bear paw print cookies | Cranberries |
| Margarine | Walnuts |
| Vegetable shortening | Pecans |
| Coconut oil | Unsweetened carob powder |
| Soy-based butter | Dark chocolate |
| Vegan butter | Semisweet chocolate chips |
| Unsweetened applesauce | Vanilla bean paste |
| Ripe banana | Vanilla powder |
| Yogurt | White chocolate chips |
| Almond milk | Butterscotch chips |
| Soy milk | Dried fruits (raisins, cranberries) |
| Oat milk | Chopped nuts (walnuts, pecans) |
| Coconut milk | Greek yoghourt |

**Regular yoghourt**
**Sour cream**
**Coconut yoghourt**
**Almond yoghourt**
**White vinegar**
**Lemon juice**
**Arrowroot powder**
**Potato starch**

## TOOLS, EQUIPMENTS AND MATERIALS

*1. Mixing Bowls:* Use a variety of mixing bowls in different sizes to prepare and combine components.

*2. Measuring Cups and Spoons:* Use accurate measuring cups and spoons to measure dry and liquid components precisely.

*3. Stand Mixer with Paddle Attachment or Hand Mixer:* Use a stand mixer with a paddle attachment or a hand mixer to blend dough and cream butter and sugar.

*4. Whisk:* Use a whisk to fully combine the dry and wet components.

*5. Rubber Spatula:* Use rubber spatulas to mix ingredients thoroughly, scrape the edges of bowls, and fold in ingredients.

*6. Baking Sheets:* For even baking and simple cookie removal, use baking sheets lined with parchment paper or silicone baking mats.

*7. Cookie scoops:* Use cookie scoops of different sizes to portion cookie dough evenly.

*8. A rolling pin:* A rolling pin is used to spread and level cookie dough.

*9. Cookie cutters:* A variety of sizes and shapes of cookie cutters are used to make different cookie designs.

*10. Cooling Racks:* Cookies can cool evenly and without getting soggy on cooling racks.

*11. Oven Thermometer:* Oven thermostats can be unreliable, so use an oven thermometer to make sure your oven is at the right temperature.

*12. Parchment paper:* Line baking trays with parchment paper to stop biscuits from sticking.

*13. Timer:* To keep track of baking times, use a timer, either a dedicated kitchen timer or the one built into your oven.

*14. Zester:* A zester is used to add citrus zest for taste to cookies.

*15. Grater:* A tool used to finely grate materials like citrus peel, almonds, and chocolate.

*16. Cooling Rack:* enables speedy and even cooling of biscuits.

*17. Cookie Decorating Tools:* You'll need piping bags, tips, and food coloring if you want to decorate cookies.

*18. Pastry Brush:* Use a pastry brush to coat cookies in egg wash or glaze.

*19. Apron and Kitchen Towels:* A kitchen towel for rapid cleanup and handling hot cookware, and an apron to keep your clothes clean.

*20. Baking mat:* A baking mat is used to gauge dough thickness and guarantee uniform rolling.

*21. Food Scale:* Use a food scale to weigh items and measure them precisely.

*22. Oven mitts or pot holders:* are used to handle hot baking sheets and pans.

*23. Baking Powder and Baking Soda Containers:* Storage containers for baking powder and baking soda fresh and clump-free.

*24. Cookie Storage Containers:* To keep baked cookies fresh, store them in airtight containers.

*25. Pastry Wheel:* Use a pastry wheel to cut cookie dough into desired shapes.

*26. Pastry Brush:* Use a pastry brush to coat cookies in melted butter, egg wash, or glaze.

*27. Wire mesh strainers:* are used to sift dry materials.

*28. Food processor (for some recipes):* For recipes that call for components that have been finely chopped or pureed, use a food processor.

*29. Kitchen scale:* Use a kitchen scale for accurate measures, especially when making recipes that call for weight.

# 30 COOKIE BAKING "MASTER" TIPS

Here are 30 cookie baking secrets and tips to ensure expert outcomes when using the "All-Continents Cookie Baking" book:

**1. Creaming Butter and Sugar:**
Beat butter and sugar together until light and fluffy, usually for 2 to 3 minutes, as directed in the recipes. Proper creaming ensures the right cookie texture.

**2. Butter Temperature:**
Use butter at the specified temperature in the recipe. Cold butter can be used if no temperature is indicated.

**3. Consistent Shape:**
Achieve uniform cookie shapes by using a cookie scoop or kitchen scale. Weigh the dough or use a scoop to portion out the correct size.

**4. Final Mixing:**
After using a stand mixer, give the dough a final mix with a spatula to ensure it's perfectly combined with no streaks or pockets of flour.

**5. Prevent Sticking:**
When flattening cookies, prevent dough from sticking to the cup by greasing a small square of parchment paper with cooking spray and placing it between the dough and the glass.

**6. Proper Pan Usage:**
Line your baking pans with parchment paper as directed, and use the correct pan size specified in the recipe to ensure even baking.

**7. Oven Accuracy:**
Check if your oven is heating properly with an oven thermometer. Uneven or inaccurate oven temperatures can lead to unevenly baked cookies.

**8. Patience Pays Off:**
Let cookies cool as directed in the recipe to achieve the perfect texture. As tempting as they may be, resist the urge to dive in right away.

**9. Preheat the Oven:**
Before baking, always warm your oven to the recommended setting. This ensures consistent results.

**10. Measuring Flour:**
When measuring flour, use the spoon-and-level method. Spoon the flour into your measuring cup and level it off with a flat edge for accurate measurements.

**11. Room Temperature Eggs:**
Use room temperature eggs for better incorporation into the dough.

**12. Fresh Ingredients:**
Use fresh and high-quality ingredients for the best flavour and texture.

**13. Properly Sized Baking Sheets:**
Use baking sheets of the appropriate size and ensure there is enough space between cookies to allow for even spreading during baking.

**14. Rotate the Pans:**

If your oven has hot spots, rotate the baking pans halfway through the baking time to ensure even cooking.

### 15. Chilling the Dough:
Follow any instructions to chill the dough before baking, as this can help prevent cookies from spreading too much.

### 16. Evenly Distributed Add-Ins:
When adding chocolate chips, nuts, or other mix-ins, ensure they are evenly distributed throughout the dough.

### 17. Parchment Paper:
Use parchment paper to line baking sheets for easy cleanup and to prevent cookies from sticking.

### 18. Softened Brown Sugar:
To soften brown sugar that has hardened, place a slice of bread or a damp paper towel in the container and seal it overnight.

### 19. Room Temperature Butter:
Allow butter to come to room temperature before starting to bake for better incorporation with other ingredients.

### 20. Sifting Dry Ingredients:
Sift flour, baking powder, and other dry ingredients to remove lumps and ensure even distribution.

### 21. Don't Overmix:
Avoid overmixing the cookie dough once the dry ingredients are added to prevent tough cookies.

### 22. Monitor Baking Time:
Keep a close eye on cookies during the final minutes of baking to prevent overbaking.

### 23. Use a Timer:
Set a timer to remind you when to check on cookies to prevent burning.

### 24. Test One Cookie First:
If you're unsure about baking time, bake one test cookie to gauge the timing before baking a whole batch.

### 25. Cooling Racks:
Use cooling racks to allow air circulation and prevent cookies from becoming soggy on the bottom.

### 26. Store Properly:
Store cookies in an airtight container to keep them fresh and maintain their texture.

### 27. Flavour Enhancers:
Enhance cookie flavours with spices, extracts, or zests as suggested in the recipes.

### 28. Cookie Variations:
Don't hesitate to experiment with ingredient substitutions and additions to create your unique cookie variations.

### 29. Record Your Experiments:
Keep a baking journal to note any modifications you make to recipes and their outcomes for future reference.

### 30. Share and Enjoy:
Finally, share your beautifully baked cookies with friends and family and enjoy the delicious results of your cookie-baking adventures!

# CONCLUSION

We've set out on an amazing voyage across the globe of cookies in the pages of "The Continental Cookie Baking," learning about the distinctive tastes, customs, and tales that each continent has to share. This book has served as a culinary passport to the sweetest regions of our globe, taking readers from the traditional American chocolate chip cookies to the exotic Thai mango sticky rice cookies.

We've discovered crucial baking tips that will guarantee perfect cookies every time. We've discovered the enchantment of accurate ingredient measures, the delight of experimenting, and the finesse of creaming butter and sugar. We have embraced the knowledge of selecting the appropriate equipment and methods, as well as the patience of allowing cookies to cool.

Remember as we draw to a conclusion that "The Continental Cookie Baking" is more than simply a cookbook; it's a method to discover many cultures via the common language of food. You join this global cookie trip by sharing your masterpieces and the tales behind them, making friends with individuals from all over the world while sharing the joy of baking.

Through the skill of cookie baking, you have the ability to create new traditions, conjure memories, and make others smile in your kitchen. So, with a freshly made cookie in hand, go forth and create, explore, and enjoy every minute. Make your kitchen a space for inspiration, comfort, and delectable discoveries.

May the world of cookies continue to inspire your culinary explorations, and may you never tire of delighting loved ones with your scrumptious creations. As you put this book away, remember that the adventure is only getting started and the world of cookies is waiting to be discovered. Happy baking, and may all the sweetest things come your way!

I appreciate you coming along on our enjoyable journey through "All-Continents Cookie Baking."

# BONUS GUIDE

# COOKIE DECORATING TECHNIQUES

## MILLY COOKWELL

# BONUS: BEGINNER'S GUIDE TO COOKIE DECORATING TECHNIQUES

The "Beginner's Guide to Cookie Decorating Techniques," a companion book to help you improve your cookie decorating abilities, is here to welcome you. By offering detailed instructions on beginner-friendly methods, we'll build on the inventive cookie-decorating advice featured in the main book in this guide to help you make wonderfully adorned cookies. Let's begin your voyage of decorating cookies!

## ROYAL ICING PIPING

Royal icing piping is a versatile technique that can add intricate and stunning designs to your cookies. Whether you're a beginner or looking to hone your skills, this step-by-step tutorial will guide you in mastering royal icing piping for cookie decoration.

**Materials You'll Need:**
- Prepared royal icing (thick consistency).
- Piping bags.
- Piping tips (various sizes for different effects).
- Couplers (for easily changing tips).
- Gel food coloring.
- Practice cookies (baked and cooled).
- Parchment paper or wax paper.
- A small bowl of clean water.
- Damp cloth or paper towels (for wiping tips).
- Toothpicks or a scribe tool (for fine details).

### Step 1: Prepare Royal Icing
Start with royal icing that is thick in consistency. If you're using store-bought royal icing mix, follow the instructions to achieve the desired thickness. For homemade royal icing, adjust the consistency by adding powdered sugar to thicken or water to thin as needed.

### Step 2: Assemble Your Piping Bag
Attach a coupler to your piping bag and select the desired piping tip. Screw it onto the coupler, ensuring it's secure.

### Step 3: Color the Icing
Divide your royal icing into smaller portions and add gel food coloring to achieve the colors you desire. Mix until the color is evenly distributed. Place each color into separate piping bags.

### Step 4: Practice Piping
Before working on your cookies, practice your piping on parchment paper. Hold the piping bag at a 45-degree angle to the paper and apply gentle pressure. Start by piping

lines, dots, and basic shapes to get a feel for the icing flow.

### Step 5: Prepare Your Cookie
Ensure your cookies are cooled and ready for decoration.

### Step 6: Start Piping
Hold the piping bag at a 45-degree angle to the cookie's surface.
Apply gentle, consistent pressure to start piping your design. Steadiness is key.
Experiment with different piping tips and techniques to create borders, flowers, lettering, or intricate details.

### Step 7: Consistency and Flow
Consistency is crucial. If the icing is too thick, it may not flow smoothly; if it's too thin, it will spread uncontrollably. Adjust the icing by adding small amounts of water to thin or powdered sugar to thicken until you achieve the desired flow.

### Step 8: Layering and Dimension
For three-dimensional effects, pipe one layer of icing and allow it to set slightly. Then, pipe additional layers or details on top. This creates dimension in your designs.

### Step 9: Let It Dry
Allow your piped designs to dry completely. This can take several hours, depending on the humidity in your environment. It's best to leave them overnight to ensure they set properly.

### Step 10: Add More Details
Once the base layers have dried, you can add fine details with contrasting colors or add more intricate piping on top.

### Step 11: Cleanup
Between color changes, wipe the tip of the piping bag with a damp cloth or paper towel to prevent color contamination.

### Step 12: Fine-Tune with a Scribe Tool
For precise adjustments, use a toothpick or a scribe tool to fine-tune your design while the icing is still wet.

### Step 13: Presentation
Once your cookies are fully decorated and dried, they're ready to be displayed or shared with family and friends.

## BUTTERCREAM PIPING

Buttercream piping is a delicious and versatile technique that can add intricate and delightful designs to your cookies. Whether you're a beginner or looking to enhance your skills, this step-by-step tutorial will guide you in mastering buttercream piping for cookie decoration.

### Materials You'll Need:
- Prepared buttercream frosting (thick consistency).
- Piping bags.
- Piping tips (various sizes for different effects).
- Couplers (for easily changing tips).
- Gel food coloring.
- Practice cookies (baked and cooled).
- Parchment paper or wax paper.
- A small bowl of clean water.

- Damp cloth or paper towels (for wiping tips).
- Toothpicks or a scribe tool (for fine details).

**Step 1: Prepare Buttercream Frosting**
Start with buttercream frosting that is thick in consistency. If using store-bought frosting, check for the desired consistency. For homemade frosting, adjust thickness by adding more powdered sugar or a splash of milk, as needed.

**Step 2: Assemble Your Piping Bag**
Attach a coupler to your piping bag and select the desired piping tip. Secure the tip onto the coupler.

**Step 3: Color the Buttercream**
Divide your buttercream frosting into smaller portions and add gel food coloring to achieve the colors you desire. Mix until the color is evenly distributed. Place each color into separate piping bags.

**Step 4: Practice Piping**
Before working on your cookies, practice your piping on parchment paper. Hold the piping bag at a 45-degree angle to the paper and apply gentle pressure. Start by piping lines, dots, and basic shapes to become familiar with the icing flow.

**Step 5: Prepare Your Cookie**
Ensure your cookies are cooled and ready for decoration.

**Step 6: Start Piping**
- Hold the piping bag at a 45-degree angle to the cookie's surface.
- Apply gentle, consistent pressure to begin piping your design. Keep your hand steady.
- Experiment with different piping tips and techniques to create borders, flowers, lettering, or intricate details.

**Step 7: Consistency and Flow**
Consistency is important. If the icing is too thick, it may not flow smoothly; if it's too thin, it will spread uncontrollably. Adjust the icing by adding small amounts of milk to thin or powdered sugar to thicken until you achieve the desired flow.

**Step 8: Layering and Dimension**
For three-dimensional effects, pipe one layer of icing and allow it to set slightly. Then, pipe additional layers or details on top. This creates depth in your designs.

**Step 9: Let It Set**
Allow your piped designs to set completely. This can take some time, depending on the humidity in your environment. Leaving them undisturbed for a few hours or overnight is ideal.

**Step 10: Add More Details**
Once the base layers have set, add fine details with contrasting colors or add more intricate piping on top.

**Step 11: Cleanup**
Between color changes, wipe the tip of the piping bag with a damp cloth or paper towel to prevent color contamination.

**Step 12: Fine-Tune with a Scribe Tool**

For precise adjustments, use a toothpick or a scribe tool to fine-tune your design while the icing is still wet.

**Step 13: Presentation**
Once your cookies are fully decorated and have set, they're ready to be displayed or shared with family and friends.

## PIPING BAG TYPES

Piping bags are essential tools for cookie decorating, allowing you to achieve precise and intricate designs. In this tutorial, we'll explore different types of piping bags and how to use them effectively for decorating your cookies.

**Materials You'll Need:**
- Piping bags (disposable or reusable).
- Couplers (for easily changing tips).
- Piping tips (various sizes for different effects).
- Prepared royal icing or buttercream frosting.
- Gel food coloring (if desired).
- Practice cookies (baked and cooled).
- Parchment paper or wax paper.
- A small bowl of clean water.
- Damp cloth or paper towels (for wiping tips).

**Step 1: Understanding Piping Bags**
Piping bags come in two primary categories: reusable and disposable.

*Disposable Piping Bags:*
- These are convenient for one-time use and save you the hassle of cleaning.
- Select the desired bag size, and cut the tip to fit your piping tip.
- Fill the bag with your prepared icing and twist the open end to seal.
- Reusable Piping Bags:

*Reusable Bags*
- Choose the size that suits your needs, and attach a coupler to the bag.
- Select the desired piping tip and secure it onto the coupler.
- Fill the bag with icing and twist the open end to seal.

**Step 2: Using Piping Bags**
- For both disposable and reusable bags, start by folding down the top of the bag about one-third of the way to create a cuff.
- Insert the desired piping tip into the bag (for reusable bags, it goes onto the coupler).
- If you're using gel food coloring, consider coloring your icing before filling the bag.
- Fill the bag with icing, leaving some space at the top to prevent overflow.
- Twist the open end of the bag to seal it and secure the icing inside.

**Step 3: Piping Techniques**
- Hold the filled bag at a 45-degree angle to the cookie's surface.
- Apply gentle, consistent pressure to the bag to start piping your design.
- Use different tips and techniques to create borders, flowers, lettering, or intricate details.

**Step 4: Cleaning Piping Bags**
- After you've completed your decorating, it's essential to clean reusable bags

thoroughly. Empty any remaining icing, and rinse the bag with warm, soapy water.
- Alternatively, you can use a dishwasher or sterilize reusable bags in boiling water.

**Step 5: Drying Piping Bags**
- For both disposable and reusable bags, make sure they are completely dry before using them again.
- Hang them or prop them open with the cuff folded down to allow air circulation.

## PIPING NOZZLES AND TIPS

Piping nozzles and tips are the heart of any successful cookie decorating endeavor. In this tutorial, we'll explore different piping nozzles and tips and how to use them effectively to achieve a wide range of stunning designs.

**Materials You'll Need:**
- Piping nozzles and tips (various types and sizes).
- Piping bags (disposable or reusable).
- Couplers (for easily changing tips).
- Prepared royal icing or buttercream frosting.
- Gel food coloring (if desired).
- Practice cookies (baked and cooled).
- Parchment paper or wax paper.
- A small bowl of clean water.
- Damp cloth or paper towels (for wiping tips).

**Step 1: Understanding Piping Nozzles and Tips**
There are numerous piping nozzle and tip shapes and sizes, each designed for specific decorative effects.

*Here are some common types:*
**Round Tips:** Create fine lines, dots, and basic shapes.
**Star Tips:** Produce stars, shells, rosettes, and borders.
**Leaf Tips:** Ideal for leaves, petals, and intricate floral designs.
**Petal Tips:** Shape delicate flower petals and ruffled edges.
**Ruffle Tips:** Create dramatic ruffles and frills.
**Basketweave Tips:** Craft basketweave patterns and lattice designs.
**Open Star Tips:** Make large, airy rosettes and swirls.
**Closed Star Tips:** Create tight, defined rosettes and swirls.
**Specialty Tips:** Form grass, fur, or other unique textures.

**Step 2: Using Piping Nozzles and Tips**
- Begin by inserting the desired piping nozzle or tip into your piping bag.
- If you're using a reusable bag, secure the tip with a coupler.
- If you plan to use different tips or colors, prepare multiple piping bags.
- Ensure the nozzle or tip is securely attached, especially for reusable bags.

**Step 3: Piping Techniques**
- Hold the filled bag at a 45-degree angle to the cookie's surface.
- Apply gentle, consistent pressure to the bag to start piping your design.
- Experiment with different nozzles and tips to create borders, flowers, lettering, or intricate details.

**Step 4: Changing Tips**

- When working with a reusable bag and coupler, it's easy to switch tips for different parts of your design.
- Simply unscrew the coupler and tip, replace with the desired tip, and secure it.

**Step 5: Cleaning Tips**
- After completing your decorating, it's important to clean your tips thoroughly.
- Rinse them with warm, soapy water or use a piping tip brush to remove any icing residue.

## PIPING BORDERS AND OUTLINES

Piping borders gives your designs a clean and polished look.

**Materials You'll Need:**
- Piping bag (disposable or reusable).
- Round or star piping tip
- Prepared royal icing or buttercream frosting.
- Gel food coloring (if desired).
- Practice cookies (baked and cooled).
- Parchment paper or wax paper.
- A small bowl of clean water.
- Damp cloth or paper towels (for wiping tips).

**Step 1: Prepare Your Icing**
- Start with the appropriate consistency of royal icing or buttercream frosting.
- For borders and outlines, a slightly thicker consistency works best.
- If your icing is too thin, add more powdered sugar to thicken it.

**Step 2: Fill Your Piping Bag**

- If you're using a disposable piping bag, cut a small opening at the tip.
- If you're using a reusable bag, attach a round or star piping tip.
- Fill your bag with the prepared icing.
- Twist the open end of the bag to seal it and secure the icing inside.

**Step 3: Practice on Parchment Paper**
- Before decorating your cookies, practice creating straight lines and curved shapes on a sheet of parchment paper.
- This will help you get a feel for the pressure needed to achieve even lines.

**Step 4: Outline Your Cookie**
- Start with a cooled cookie.
- Hold the piping bag at a 45-degree angle to the cookie's surface.
- Apply even pressure to the bag and pipe along the edge of the cookie, creating an outline.
- For borders, you can pipe a second line inside the first one, or create scalloped edges.
- If you make a mistake, you can gently lift the icing off the cookie using a toothpick.

**Step 5: Flooding the Center**
Once you've created an outline, you can use a thinner consistency of icing (flood icing) to fill the center of the cookie. This will create a smooth, clean surface inside the border or outline.

**Step 6: Let It Dry**
- Allow the icing to set completely before adding additional decorations or details. This can take several hours, or you can leave the cookies to dry overnight.

**Step 7: Add More Details**
Once the base layer has set, you can add more intricate details, such as flowers, letters, or other designs within the outlined area.

**Step 8: Cleanup**
Wipe the piping tip with a damp cloth or paper towel between color changes to prevent color contamination.

# FLOOD AND FILL TECHNIQUE

The flood and fill technique allows you to create smooth and even backgrounds and add dimension to your designs.

**Materials You'll Need:**
- Piping bags (disposable or reusable).
- Round or star piping tip
- Prepared flood icing (thinner consistency).
- Prepared royal icing or buttercream frosting for outline (thicker consistency).
- Gel food coloring (if desired).
- Practice cookies (baked and cooled).
- Parchment paper or wax paper.
- A small bowl of clean water.
- Damp cloth or paper towels (for wiping tips).

**Step 1: Prepare Your Icing**
- Start by preparing two consistencies of icing:
- Flood Icing: Thinner consistency, similar to the texture of shampoo. Add a little water to thin it out if it's too thick.
- Outline Icing: Thicker consistency, suitable for creating borders and outlines.

**Step 2: Fill Your Piping Bags**
- Use a disposable piping bag for each type of icing. Cut a small opening at the tip of the flood icing bag.
- Attach a round or star piping tip to the reusable bag for outline icing.
- Fill the bags with their respective icings.
- Twist the open ends of the bags to seal them and secure the icing inside.

**Step 3: Outline Your Cookie**
- Start with a cooled cookie.
- Hold the piping bag with the outline icing at a 45-degree angle to the cookie's surface.
- Apply even pressure to the bag and pipe an outline around the edge of the cookie.

**Step 4: Fill the Center with Flood Icing**
- Once the outline has set slightly (but not completely), use the flood icing to fill the center of the cookie.
- Start by piping a line of flood icing just inside the outline.
- Use a toothpick or scribe tool to guide the icing into any corners or small areas.

**Step 5: Use a Toothpick for Smoothing**

- Gently shake or tap the cookie to help the flood icing settle and create an even surface.
- Use a toothpick or scribe tool to guide the icing into any areas that need filling or smoothing.
- Be careful not to press too hard and disrupt the outline.

**Step 6: Let It Dry**
- Allow the icing to dry completely before adding additional decorations or details.

97

This can take several hours or be left to dry overnight.

### Step 7: Add More Details
Once the base layer has set, you can add more intricate details, such as flowers, letters, or other designs on top of the flooded area.

### Step 8: Cleanup
Wipe the piping tip with a damp cloth or paper towel between color changes to prevent color contamination.

## ROYAL ICING FLOODING

Flooding with royal icing helps achieve smooth and even backgrounds and add dimension to your cookie designs.

### Materials You'll Need:
- Piping bags (disposable or reusable).
- Round or star piping tip
- Prepared flood icing (thinner consistency)
- Prepared royal icing for outline (thicker consistency)
- Gel food coloring (if desired).
- Practice cookies (baked and cooled).
- Parchment paper or wax paper.
- A small bowl of clean water.
- Damp cloth or paper towels (for wiping tips).

### Step 1: Prepare Your Icing
- Start by preparing two consistencies of icing:
- Flood Icing: Thinner consistency, similar to the texture of shampoo.
- Add little quantities of water to thin it if it's too thick.
- Outline Icing: Thicker consistency, suitable for creating borders and outlines.

### Step 2: Fill Your Piping Bags
- Use a disposable piping bag for each type of icing.
- Cut a small opening at the tip of the flood icing bag.
- Attach a round or star piping tip to the reusable bag for outline icing.
- Fill the bags with their respective icings.
- Twist the open ends of the bags to seal them and secure the icing inside.

### Step 3: Outline Your Cookie
- Start with a cooled cookie.
- Hold the piping bag with the outline icing at a 45-degree angle to the cookie's surface.
- Apply even pressure to the bag and pipe an outline around the edge of the cookie.

### Step 4: Flood the Center with Royal Icing
- Once the outline has set slightly (but not completely), use the flood icing to fill the center of the cookie.
- Start by piping a line of flood icing just inside the outline.
- Use a toothpick or scribe tool to guide the icing into any corners or small areas.

### Step 5: Use a Toothpick for Smoothing
- Gently shake or tap the cookie to help the flood icing settle and create an even surface.
- Use a toothpick or scribe tool to guide the icing into any areas that need filling or smoothing.
- Be careful not to press too hard and disrupt the outline.

### Step 6: Let It Dry

- Allow the icing to dry completely before adding additional decorations or details.
- This can take several hours or be left to dry overnight.

**Step 7: Add More Details**
Once the base layer has set, you can add more intricate details, such as flowers, letters, or other designs on top of the flooded area.

**Step 8: Cleanup**
Wipe the piping tip with a damp cloth or paper towel between color changes to prevent color contamination.

# GLAZE FLOODING

Glaze flooding is an alternative technique to royal icing flooding, offering a glossy, translucent finish. In this tutorial, we'll explore how to master glaze flooding to create beautifully decorated cookies with a unique look.

**Materials You'll Need:**
- Piping bags (disposable or reusable).
- Round or star piping tip
- Prepared glaze icing (thinner consistency).
- Prepared royal icing for outline (thicker consistency).
- Gel food coloring (if desired).
- Practice cookies (baked and cooled).
- Parchment paper or wax paper.
- A small bowl of clean water.
- Damp cloth or paper towels (for wiping tips).

**Step 1: Prepare Your Icing**
- Start by preparing two consistencies of icing:
- Glaze Icing: Thinner consistency, similar to the texture of shampoo.
- Add little quantities of water to thin it if it's too thick.
- Outline Icing: Thicker consistency, suitable for creating borders and outlines.

**Step 2: Fill Your Piping Bags**
- Use a disposable piping bag for each type of icing.
- Cut a small opening at the tip of the glaze icing bag.
- Attach a round or star piping tip to the reusable bag for outline icing.
- Fill the bags with their respective icings.
- Twist the open ends of the bags to seal them and secure the icing inside.

**Step 3: Outline Your Cookie**
- Start with a cooled cookie.
- Hold the piping bag with the outline icing at a 45-degree angle to the cookie's surface.
- Apply even pressure to the bag and pipe an outline around the edge of the cookie.

**Step 4: Flood the Center with Glaze Icing**
- Once the outline has set slightly (but not completely), use the glaze icing to fill the center of the cookie.
- Start by piping a line of glaze icing just inside the outline.
- Use a toothpick or scribe tool to guide the icing into any corners or small areas.

**Step 5: Use a Toothpick for Smoothing**
- Gently shake or tap the cookie to help the glaze icing settle and create an even surface.
- Use a toothpick or scribe tool to guide the icing into any areas that need filling or smoothing.

- Be careful not to press too hard and disrupt the outline.

**Step 6: Let It Dry**
- Allow the icing to dry completely before adding additional decorations or details.
- Glaze icing dries with a glossy finish, creating a unique effect on your cookies.

**Step 7: Add More Details**
- Once the base layer has set, you can add more intricate details, such as flowers, letters, or other designs on top of the glazed area.

**Step 8: Cleanup**
Wipe the piping tip with a damp cloth or paper towel between color changes to prevent color contamination.

# CREATING DIMENSION WITH FLOODING

Creating dimension with flooding is a technique that adds depth and visual interest to your cookie designs.

**Materials You'll Need:**
- Piping bags (disposable or reusable).
- Round or star piping tip
- Prepared flood icing (thinner consistency).
- Prepared royal icing or buttercream frosting for outline (thicker consistency).
- Gel food coloring (if desired).
- Practice cookies (baked and cooled).
- Parchment paper or wax paper.
- A small bowl of clean water.
- Damp cloth or paper towels (for wiping tips).

**Step 1: Prepare Your Icing**
- Start by preparing two consistencies of icing:
- Flood Icing: Thinner consistency, similar to the texture of shampoo.
- If it's too thick, add small amounts of water to thin it.
- Outline Icing: Thicker consistency, suitable for creating borders and outlines.

**Step 2: Fill Your Piping Bags**
- Use a disposable piping bag for each type of icing.
- Cut a small opening at the tip of the flood icing bag.
- Attach a round or star piping tip to the reusable bag for outline icing.
- Fill the bags with their respective icings.
- Twist the open ends of the bags to seal them and secure the icing inside.

**Step 3: Outline Your Cookie**
- Start with a cooled cookie.
- Hold the piping bag with the outline icing at a 45-degree angle to the cookie's surface.
- Apply even pressure to the bag and pipe an outline around the edge of the cookie.

**Step 4: Flood the Center with Royal Icing**
- Once the outline has set slightly (but not completely), use the flood icing to fill the center of the cookie.
- Start by piping a line of flood icing just inside the outline.
- Use a toothpick or scribe tool to guide the icing into any corners or small areas.

**Step 5: Layer with Different Consistencies**
- To create dimension, allow the initial flood icing layer to set slightly, but not fully.

- Then, pipe additional details or decorations using a slightly thicker consistency of icing. This will add depth to your design.

**Step 6: Use a Toothpick for Smoothing**
- Gently shake or tap the cookie to help the icing settle and create an even surface.
- Use a toothpick or scribe tool to guide the icing into any areas that need filling or smoothing.
- Be careful not to press too hard and disrupt the outline.

**Step 7: Let It Dry**
- Allow the icing to dry completely before adding additional decorations or details.
- This can take several hours or be left to dry overnight.

**Step 8: Cleanup**
- Wipe the piping tip with a damp cloth or paper towel between color changes to prevent color contamination.

## FIXING FLOODED COOKIES

Mistakes happen, and it's essential to know how to fix flooded cookies when things don't go as planned. In this section, we'll explore some common issues that can occur during cookie flooding and how to rectify them to salvage your beautifully decorated treats.

**Materials You'll Need:**
- Flooded cookies with issues.
- Prepared flood icing (thinner consistency).
- Toothpicks or scribe tool.
- Paper towels.

## Common Issues and How to Fix Them:

**1. Air Bubbles:**
*Issue:* Small air bubbles can sometimes form in your flooded icing.

*Fix:* Use a toothpick or scribe tool to gently pop the air bubbles. Once popped, smooth out the icing around the area.

**2. Uneven or Missing Icing:**
*Issue:* You may find that your flood icing didn't spread evenly, or there are gaps.

*Fix:* Add a small amount of flood icing to the affected area, and use a toothpick or scribe tool to spread and blend it with the existing icing.

**3. Overflowing Icing:**
*Issue:* If your flood icing has overflowed beyond the cookie's edge, it can create a messy appearance.

*Fix:* While the icing is still wet, use a clean paper towel to gently blot and absorb the excess icing. Be careful not to remove too much or disrupt the design.

**4. Color Bleeding:**
*Issue:* Sometimes, different colors of icing can bleed into each other, causing color contamination.

*Fix:* To prevent color bleeding, ensure that each color is fully dry before adding the next. If it has already occurred, let the icing dry, then add a small border or decorative element to cover the affected area.

### 5. Streaks or Uneven Surfaces:
*Issue:* Your flooded icing may not have settled smoothly, leaving streaks or uneven surfaces.

*Fix:* While the icing is still wet, use a toothpick or scribe tool to gently smooth and blend the surface until it appears even.

### 6. Craters or Holes:
*Issue:* Sometimes, small craters or holes can appear in your flooded icing.

*Fix:* Fill the craters or holes with additional flood icing, and use a toothpick or scribe tool to smooth the surface.

### 7. Smudged Outline:
*Issue:* If your outline icing smudged into your flood icing, it can affect the design's clarity.

*Fix:* Let the icing dry, and then use a clean paper towel to gently rub off the smudged area. You can also add a thin border or design element to cover the smudge.

## Fixing Royal Icing Mistakes for Cookie Decorating

Even the most experienced cookie decorators make mistakes with royal icing from time to time. Knowing how to fix these errors can help salvage your beautifully decorated cookies. In this section, we'll explore common royal icing mistakes and how to rectify them.

**Materials You'll Need:**
- Cookies with royal icing mistakes.
- Prepared royal icing for repair (thicker consistency).
- A small piping bag with a fine round or star tip.
- Toothpicks or scribe tool.
- Parchment paper or wax paper.

## COMMON ROYAL ICING MISTAKES AND HOW TO FIX THEM:

### 1. Smudged or Blurred Lines:
*Mistake:* Your royal icing lines have smudged or blurred into each other.

*Fix:* Allow the icing to dry completely. Once dry, use a clean toothpick or scribe tool to gently scrape away the smudged icing. Be cautious not to damage the underlying layer. Afterward, you can re-pipe the lines.

### 2. Cracks in the Icing:
*Mistake:* You notice cracks or gaps in your dried royal icing.

*Fix:* Prepare a thicker consistency of royal icing. Using a small piping bag fitted with a fine round or star tip, pipe a small amount of this icing into the cracks or gaps. Use a toothpick or scribe tool to smooth and blend the icing until the surface appears even.

### 3. Color Bleeding:

*Mistake:* Different colors of royal icing have bled into each other, causing color contamination.

*Fix:* To prevent color bleeding, ensure that each color is fully dry before adding the next. If bleeding has already occurred, let the icing dry, and then add a small border or decorative element to cover the affected area.

### 4. Icing Drips:
*Mistake:* Drips of royal icing have occurred where you didn't intend.

*Fix:* Let the drips dry completely. Once dry, you can either scrape them away gently with a toothpick or scribe tool or use a thicker consistency of royal icing to add a decorative element that incorporates the drips.

### 5. Over-Piping:
*Mistake:* You've piped more details or icing than you intended, making the design too crowded.

*Fix:* Let the icing dry. Once dry, you can carefully scrape away or remove the excess icing with a toothpick or scribe tool. You can also adjust your design to incorporate the additional details.

### 6. Smudged Outline:
*Mistake:* If your outline icing smudged into the flooded area, it can affect the design's clarity.

*Fix:* Let the icing dry, and then use a clean toothpick or scribe tool to gently rub off the smudged area. You can also add a thin border or design element to cover the smudge.

# HANDLING HUMIDITY IN COOKIE DECORATING

Humidity can be a challenge for cookie decorators, as it affects the consistency and drying time of icing. In this tutorial, we'll explore how to handle humidity and create beautifully decorated cookies even in less-than-ideal conditions.

**Materials You'll Need:**
Prepared royal icing (flood and outline consistency).
Prepared cookies (baked and cooled).
Parchment paper or wax paper.
A dehumidifier or air conditioner (optional).
A small fan (optional).
A clean, dry workspace.

**Step 1: Monitor Humidity Levels**
Start by monitoring the humidity levels in your decorating area. A hygrometer may be used to measure humidity precisely.

**Step 2: Adjust Icing Consistency**
If the humidity is high, you'll need to thicken your royal icing by adding more powdered sugar. High humidity can make icing too thin and slow the drying process.

**Step 3: Drying Cookies**
- Ensure your cookies are thoroughly cooled before decorating.

- If they're even slightly warm, the icing can become runny in humid conditions.

### Step 4: Use a Dehumidifier or Air Conditioner
If the humidity is excessive, consider using a dehumidifier or air conditioner to reduce the moisture in the room. This can help the icing dry faster and maintain its shape.

### Step 5: Place a Fan Nearby
- Setting up a small fan near your decorated cookies can help circulate the air and speed up the drying process.
- Ensure it's not blowing directly onto the cookies to prevent the icing from drying unevenly.

### Step 6: Work in Smaller Batches
In highly humid conditions, work in smaller batches to prevent your icing from becoming too runny before you've finished decorating. This can be especially helpful when using different colors.

### Step 7: Use a Desiccant Pack
Placing a desiccant pack in an airtight container with your undecorated cookies can help absorb excess moisture and prevent the cookies from becoming soft.

### Step 8: Plan Adequate Drying Time
Allow more time for the cookies to dry in high humidity. It may take longer for the icing to set completely.

### Step 9: Be Patient and Mindful
Humidity can be frustrating, but it's essential to remain patient and mindful when decorating cookies in such conditions. Don't rush the procedure; rather, take your time.

# STORING DECORATED COOKIES

Storing decorated cookies is crucial to maintain their appearance, flavor, and texture. In this section, we'll explore how to properly store your beautifully decorated cookies to keep them fresh and delightful.

**Materials You'll Need:**
- Decorated cookies.
- Parchment paper or wax paper.
- Airtight containers or cookie tins.
- Plastic wrap or cellophane bags.
- Desiccant packs (optional).
- An airtight cookie jar (optional).

### Step 1: Allow Cookies to Fully Dry
Ensure that the decorated cookies have fully dried and set before storing them. Royal icing or glaze icing can take several hours or even overnight to dry completely.

### Step 2: Layer with Parchment Paper
Place a sheet of parchment paper or wax paper between each layer of decorated cookies. This prevents the cookies from sticking to each other and preserves their designs.

### Step 3: Use Airtight Containers or Cookie Tins
- Place the decorated cookies in airtight containers or cookie tins.
- Ensure that the containers have a secure

seal to prevent air and moisture from entering.

### Step 4: Add Desiccant Packs (Optional)
If you live in a particularly humid area, consider placing desiccant packs in the storage container to absorb excess moisture. This helps prevent the cookies from becoming soft or the icing from becoming sticky.

### Step 5: Seal with Plastic Wrap or Cellophane Bags
- If your cookies are individually decorated and not layered, you can wrap each cookie in plastic wrap or cellophane bags.
- Make sure they are sealed tightly to maintain freshness.

### Step 6: Keep in a Dry, Cool Place
- Store your containers or cookie tins in a cool, dry place.
- Avoid areas with direct sunlight or extreme temperature fluctuations, as these can affect the appearance and texture of the cookies.

### Step 7: Use an Airtight Cookie Jar (Optional)
If you have an airtight cookie jar, you can store your cookies in it, ensuring they remain protected from air and moisture. Displaying your beautifully decorated cookies in a cookie jar can be a charming and convenient option.

### Step 8: Rotate and Check Cookies
- Periodically check your stored cookies to ensure their freshness.
- If you notice any signs of moisture or softening, you can replace the parchment paper or desiccant packs as needed.

# COMBATING COLOR BLEEDING

Color bleeding can be a common issue when decorating cookies with different colored royal icing or flood icing. In this section, we'll explore how to prevent and combat color bleeding to maintain the crisp and vibrant appearance of your beautifully decorated cookies.

**Materials You'll Need:**
- Decorated cookies with color bleeding.
- Prepared royal icing or flood icing in the same color as the bleeding.
- Piping bags.
- Round or star piping tip
- A toothpick or scribe tool.
- Parchment paper or wax paper.

### Step 1: Identify the Bleeding Area
Carefully inspect the decorated cookies to identify the areas where color bleeding has occurred. It may appear as a blurry or smudged edge between different icing colors.

### Step 2: Prepare Matching Icing
- Prepare royal icing or flood icing in the same color as the one that bled.
- Ensure it's the correct consistency for your needs.

### Step 3: Use a Piping Bag
Fill a piping bag with the prepared icing, and attach a round or star piping tip

**Step 4: Repair the Bleeding Area**
- Gently pipe over the bleeding area with the matching icing.
- Use even pressure to create a clean, sharp edge or outline.

**Step 5: Smooth and Blend**
- Use a toothpick or scribe tool to smooth and blend the fresh icing with the surrounding area. This helps the color bleeding blend seamlessly with the rest of the design.

**Step 6: Allow to Dry**
Let the repaired area dry completely. The fresh icing should set and match the appearance of the surrounding icing.

**Step 7: Optional - Add Additional Details**
If the repaired area is part of a larger design, you can add any additional details or decorations on top of the fresh icing once it has dried.

**Step 8: Prevent Future Color Bleeding**
To prevent color bleeding in future projects, ensure that each color of icing is fully dry before adding the next. This helps maintain the crispness of your designs.

**THE END**

## OTHER BOOKS ON OUR SHELF

Weight Watchers Cookbook for Diabetics

Heart Healthy Recipes Cookbook for Seniors

The Ultimate Crockpot Cookbook for College Students

## AUTHOR'S REQUEST FOR FEEDBACK

**As part of our quest to produce ONLY quality books for reader's consumption, we deem it a great pleasure to receive your precious feedback in the reviews. Thank you for being part of our cause!**

Printed in Great Britain
by Amazon